# In the Riding-School: Chats With Esmeralda

## Theo. Stephenson Browne

In the Riding-School

Chats with Esmeralda

by Theo. Stephenson Browne

1890

—We two will ride,
Lady mine,
At your pleasure, side by side,
Laugh and chat.
ALDRICH

TO THE MODERN MEN OF UZ; MY FRENCH, ENGLISH, AND
AMERICAN MASTERS.

# CONTENTS

## I.

Impatient to mount and ride.
  *Longfellow.*

And you want to learn how to ride, Esmeralda?

Why? Because? Reason good and sufficient, Esmeralda; to require anything more definite would be brutal, although an explanation of your motives would render the task of directing you much easier.

As you are an American, it is reasonable to presume that you desire to learn quickly; as you are youthful, it is certain that you earnestly wish to look pretty in the saddle, and as you are a youthful American, there is not a shadow of a doubt that your objections to authoritative teaching will be almost unconquerable, and that you will insist upon being treated, from the very beginning, as if your small head contained the knowledge of a Hiram Woodruff or of an Archer. Perhaps you may find a teacher who will comply with your wishes; who will be exceedingly deferential to your little whims; will unhesitatingly accept your report of your own sensations and your hypotheses as to their cause; and, Esmeralda, when once your eyes behold that model man, be content, and go and take lessons of another, for either he is a pretentious humbug, careless of everything except his fees, or he is an ignoramus.

It may not be necessary that you should be insulted or ridiculed in order to become a rider, although there are girls who seem utterly impervious by teaching by gentle methods. Is it not a matter of tradition that Queen Victoria owes her regal carriage to the rough drill-sergeant who, with no effect upon his pupil, horrified her governess, and astonished her, by sharply saying: "A pretty Queen you'll make with that dot-and-go-one gait!" Up went the little chin, back went the shoulders, down went the elbows, and, in her wrath, the little princess did precisely what the old soldier had been striving to make her do; but his delighted cry of "Just right!" was a surprise to her, inasmuch as she had been conscious of no muscular effort whatsoever. From that time forth, *incessit regina*.

You may not need such rough treatment, but it is necessary that you should be corrected every moment and almost every second until you learn to correct yourself, until every muscle in your body becomes self-conscious, and until an improper position is almost instantly felt as uncomfortable, and the teacher who does not drill you steadily and continuously, permits you to fall into bad habits.

If you were a German princess, Esmeralda, you would be compelled to sit in the saddle for many an hour without touching the reins, while your patient horse walked around a tan bark ring, and you balanced yourself and straightened yourself, and adjusted arms, shoulders, waist, knees and feet, under the orders of a drill-sergeant, who might, indeed, sugar-coat his phrases with "Your Highness," but whose intonations would say "You must," as plainly as if he were drilling an awkward squad of peasant recruits. If you were the daughter of a hundred earls, you would be mounted on a Shetland pony and shaken into a good seat long before you outgrew short frocks, and afterwards you would be trained by your mother or older sisters, by the gentlemen of your family, or perhaps, by some trusted old groom, or in a good London riding-school, and, no matter who your instructor might be, you would be compelled to be submissive and obedient.

But you object that you cannot afford to pay for very careful, minute, and long-continued training; that you must content yourself with such teaching as you can obtain by riding in a ring under the charge of two or three masters, receiving such instruction as they find time to give you while maintaining order and looking after an indefinite number of other pupils. Your real teacher in that case must be yourself, striving assiduously to obey every order given to you, no matter whether it appears unreasonable or seems, as the Concord young woman said, "in accordance with the latest scientific developments and the esoteric meaning of differentiated animal existences." That sentence, by the way, silenced her master, and nearly caused him to have a fit of illness from suppression of language, but perhaps it might affect your teacher otherwise, and you would better reserve it for that private mental rehearsal of your first lesson which you will conduct in your maiden meditation.

You are your own best teacher, you understand, and you may be encouraged to know that one of the foremost horsemen in the country says: "I have had many teachers, but my best master was here," touching his forehead. "Where do you ride, sir?" asked one of his pupils, after vainly striving with reins and whip, knee, heel and spur to execute a movement which the master had compelled his horse to perform while apparently holding himself as rigid as bronze. "I ride here, sir," was the grim answer, with another tap on the forehead.

And first, Esmeralda, being feminine, you wish to know what you are to wear.

Until you have taken at least ten lessons, it would be simply foolishness for you to buy any special thing to wear, except a plain flannel skirt, the material for which should not cost you more than two dollars and a half. Harper's Bazar has published two or three patterns, following which any dressmaker can make a skirt quite good enough for the ring. A jersey, a Norfolk jacket, a simple street jacket or even an ordinary basque waist; any small, close-fitting hat, securely pinned to your hair, and very loose gloves will complete a dress quite suitable for private lessons, and not so expensive that you need grudge the swift destruction certain to come to all equestrian costumes. Nothing is more ludicrous than to see a rider clothed in a correct habit, properly scant and unhemmed, to avoid all risks when taking fences and hedges in a hunting country, with her chimney-pot hat and her own gold-mounted crop, her knowing little riding-boots and buckskins, with outfit enough for Baby Blake and Di Vernon and Lady Gay Spanker, and to see that young woman dancing in the saddle, now here and now there, pulling at the reins in a manner to make a rocking-horse rear, and squealing tearfully and jerkily: "Oh, ho-ho-oh, wh-h-hat m-m-makes h-h-him g-g-go s-s-s-so?"

If you think it possible that you may be easily discouraged, and that your first appearance in the riding-school will be your last, you need not buy any skirt, for you will find several in the school dressing-room, and, for once, you may submit to wearing a garment not your own. Shall you buy trousers or tights? Wait till you decide to take lessons before buying either, first to avoid unnecessary expense, and second, because until experience shall show what kind of a horsewoman you are likely to be, you cannot tell which will be the more suitable and comfortable. Laced boots, a plain, dark underskirt, cut princess, undergarments without a wrinkle, and no tight bands to compress veins, or to restrain muscles by adding their resistance to the force of gravitation make up the list of details to which you must give your attention before leaving home. If you be addicted to light gymnastics you will find it beneficial to practise a few movements daily, both before taking your first lesson and as long as you may continue to ride.

First—Hold your shoulders square and perfectly rigid, and turn the head towards the right four times, and then to the left four times.

Second—Bend the head four times to the right and four times to the left.

Third—Bend the head four times to the back and four times to the front. These exercises will enable you to look at anything which may interest you, without distracting the attention of your horse, as you might do if you moved your shoulders, and thus disturbed your equilibrium on your back. Feeling the change, he naturally supposes that you want something of him, and when you become as sensitive as you should be, you will notice that at such times he changes his gait perceptibly.

Fourth—Bend from the waist four times to the right, four to the left, four times forward, and four times backward. These movements will not only make the waist more flexible, but will strengthen certain muscles of the leg.

Fifth—Execute any movement which experience has shown you will square your shoulders and flatten your back most effectually. Throw the hands backward until they touch one another, or bring your elbows together behind you, if you can. Hold the arms close to the side, the elbows against the waist, the forearm at right angles with the arm, the fists clenched, with the little finger down and the knuckles facing each other, and describe ellipses, first with one shoulder, then with the other, then with both. This movement is found in Mason's School Gymnastics, and is prescribed by M. de Bussigny in his little manual for horsewomen, and it will prove admirable in its effects. Stretch the arms at full length above the head, the palms of the hands at front, the thumbs touching one another, and then carry them straight outward without bending the elbows, and bend them down, the palms still in front, until the little finger touches the leg. This movement is recommended by Mason and also by Blaikie, and as it is part of the West Point "setting up" drill, it may be regarded as considered on good authority to be efficacious in producing an erect carriage. Stand as upright as you can, your arms against your side, the forearm at right angles, as before, and jerk your elbows downward four times.

Sixth—Sit down on the floor with your feet stretched straight before you, and resting on their heels, and drop backward until you are lying flat, then resume your first position, keeping your arms and forearms at right angles during the whole exercise. Still sitting, bend as far to the right as you can, then bend as far as possible to the left, resuming a perfectly erect position between the movements, and keeping your feet and legs still. Rising, stand on your toes and let yourself down fifty times; then stand on your heels, and raise and lower your toes fifty times. The firmer you hold your arms and hands during these movements, the better for you, Esmeralda, and for the horse who will be your first victim.

Already one can seem to see him, poor, innocent beast, miserable in the memories of an army of beginners, his mouth so accustomed to being jerked in every direction, without anything in particular being meant by it, that neither Arabia nor Mexico can furnish a bit which would surprise him, or startle his four legs from their propriety. No cow is more placid, no lamb more gentle; he would not harm a tsetse fly or kick a snapping terrier. His sole object in life is to keep himself and his rider out of danger, and to betake himself to that part of the ring in which the least labor should be expected of him. The tiny girls who ride him call him "dear old Billy Buttons," or "darling Gypsy," or "nice Sir Archer." Heaven knows what he calls them in his heart! Were he human, it would be something to be expressed by dashes and "d's"; but, being a horse, he is silent, and shows his feelings principally by heading for the mounting-stand whenever he thinks that a pupil's hour is at an end.

Why that long face, Esmeralda? Must you do all those exercises? Bless your innocent soul, no! Dress yourself and run away. The exercises will be good for you, but they are not absolutely necessary. Remember, however, that your best riding-school master is behind your own pretty forehead, and that your brain can save your muscles many a strain and many a pound of labor. And remember, too, that, in riding, as in everything else, to him that hath shall be given, and the harder and firmer your muscles when you begin, the greater will be the benefit which you will derive from your rides, and the more you will enjoy them. The pale and weary invalid may gain flesh and color with every lesson, but the bright and healthy pupil, whose muscles are like iron, whose heart and lungs are in perfect order, can ride for hours without weariness, and double her strength in a comparatively short time.

But—Esmeralda, dear, before you go—whisper! Why do you want to take riding lessons? Theodore asked you to go out with him next Monday, and Nell said that she would lend you her habit, and you thought that you would take three lessons and learn to ride? There, go and dress, child; go and dress!

II.

Bring forth the horse!
  *Byron.*

Being ready to start, Esmeralda, the question now arises: "Is a riding school," as the girl asked about the new French play, "a place to which one can take her mother?" Little girls too young to dress themselves should be attended by their mothers or by their maids, but an older girl no more needs guardianship at riding-school than at any other place at which she receives instruction, and there is no more reason why her mother should follow her into the ring than into the class-room.

Her presence, even if she preserve absolute silence, will probably embarrass both teacher and pupil, and although her own children may not be affected by it, it will be decidedly troublesome to the children of other mothers.

If, instead of being quiet, she talk, and it is the nature of the mother who accompanies her daughter to riding-school to talk volubly and loudly, she will become a nuisance, and even a source of actual danger, by distracting the attention of the master from his pupils, and the attention of the pupils from their horses, to say nothing of the possibility that some of her pretty, ladylike screams of, "Oh, darling, I know you're tired!" or, "Oh, what a horrid horse; see him jump!" may really frighten some lucky animal whose acquaintance has included no women but the sensible.

If she be inclined to laugh at the awkward beginners, and to ridicule them audibly—but really, Esmeralda, it should not be necessary to consider such an action, impossible in a well-bred woman, unlikely in a woman of good feeling! Leave your mother, if not at home, in the dressing-room or the reception room, and go to the mounting-stand alone.

In some schools you may ride at any time, but the usual morning hours for ladies' lessons are from nine o'clock to noon, and the afternoon hours from two o'clock until four. Some masters prefer that their pupils should have fixed days and hours for their lessons, and others allow the very largest liberty. For your own sake it is better to have a regular time for your lessons, but if you cannot manage to do so, do not complain if you sometimes have to wait a few minutes for your horse, or for your master.

The school is not carried on entirely for your benefit, although you will at first assume that it is. As a rule, a single lesson will cost two dollars, but a ten-lesson ticket will cost but fifteen dollars, a twenty-lesson ticket twenty-five dollars, and a ticket for twenty exercise rides twenty dollars. In schools which give music-rides, there are special rates for the evenings upon which they take place, but you need not think of music-rides until you have had at least the three lessons which you desire.

Buy your ticket before you go to the dressing-room, and ask if you may have a key to a locker. Dress as quickly as you can, and if there be no maid in the dressing-room, lock up your street clothing and keep your key. If there be a maid, she will attend to this matter, and will assist you in putting on your skirt, showing you that it buttons on the left side, and that you must pin it down the basque of your jersey or your jacket in the back, unless you desire it to wave wildly with every leap of your horse. Flatter not yourself that lead weights will prevent this! When a horse begins a canter that sends you, if your feelings be any gauge, eighteen good inches nearer the ceiling, do you think that an ounce of lead will remain stationary? give a final touch to your hairpins and hatpins, button your gloves, pull the rubber straps of your habit over your right toe and left heel, and you are ready.

In most schools, you will be made to mount from the ground, and you will find it surprisingly and delightfully easy to you. What it may be to the master who puts you into the saddle is another matter, but nine out of ten teachers will make no complaint, and will assure you that they do very well.

If you wish to deceive any other girl's inconsiderate mother whom you may find comfortably seated in a good position for criticism, and to make her suppose that you are an old rider, keep silence. Do not criticise your horse or his equipments, do not profess inability to mount, but when you master says "Now!" step forward and stand facing in the same direction of your horse, placing your right hand on the upper pommel of the two on the left of the saddle.

Set your left foot in whichever hand he holds out for it. Some masters offer the left, some the right, and some count for a pupil, and others prefer that she should count for yourself. The usual "One, two, three!" means, one, rest the weight strongly on the right foot; two, bend the right knee, keeping the body perfectly erect; three, spring up from the right foot, turning very slightly to the left, so as to place yourself sideways on the saddle, your right hand toward the horse's head.

Some masters offer a shoulder as a support for a pupil's left hand, and some face toward the horse's head and some toward his tail, so it is best for you to wait a little for directions, Esmeralda, and not to suppose that, because you know all about Lucy Fountain's way of mounting a horse, or about James Burdock's tuition of Mabel Vane, there is no other method of putting a lady in the saddle.

After your first lesson, you will find it well to practise springing upward from the right foot, holding your left on a hassock, or a chair rung, your right hand raised as if grasping the pommel, your shoulders carefully kept back, and your body straight. It is best to perform this exercise before a mirror, and when you begin to think you have mastered it, close you eyes, give ten upward springs and then look at yourself. A hopeless wreck, eh? Not quite so bad as that, but, before, you unconsciously corrected your position by the eye, and you must learn to do it entirely by feeling. You will probably improve very much on a second trial, because your shoulders will begin to be sensitive. Why not practise this exercise before your first lesson? Because you should know just how your master prefers to stand, in order to be able to imagine him standing as he really will. It is not unusual to see riders of some experience puzzled and made awkward by an innovation on what they have regarded as the true and only method of mounting, although, when once the right leg and wrist are properly trained, a woman ought to be able to reach the saddle without caring what her escort's method of assistance.

Mounting from a high horseblock is a matter of being fairly lifted into the saddle, and you cannot possibly do it improperly. it is easy, but it gives you no training for rides outside the school, and masters use it, not because they approve of it, but because their pupils, not knowing how easy it is to mount from the ground, often desire it.

But, being in the saddle, turn so as to face your horse's head, put our right knee over the pommel, and slip your left foot into the stirrup. Then rise on your left foot and smooth your skirt, a task in which your master will assist you, and take you reins and your whip from him.

How shall you hold your reins? As your master tells you! Probably, he will give you but one rein at first, and very likely will direct you to hold it in both hands, keeping them five or six inches apart, the wrists on a level with the elbows or even a very little lower, and he is not likely to insist on any other details, knowing that it will be difficult for you to attain perfection in these. An English master might give you a single rein to be passed outside the little finger, and between the forefinger and the middle finger, the loop coming between the forefinger and thumb, and being held in place by the thumb. Then he would expect you to keep your right shoulder back very firmly, but a French master will tell you that it is better to learn to keep the shoulder back a little while holding a rein in the right hand, and an American master will usually allow you to take your choice, but, until you have experience, obey orders in silence.

And now, having taken your whip, draw yourself back in your saddle so as to feel the pommel under your right knee; sit well towards the right, square your shoulders, force your elbows well down, hollow your waist a little, and start. He won't go? Of course he will not, until bidden to do so, if he know his business. Bend forward the least bit in the world, draw very slightly on the reins, and rather harder on the right, so as to turn him from the stand, and away he walks, and you are in the ring. You had no idea that it was so large, and you feel as if lost on a western prairie, but you are in no danger whatsoever. You cannot fall off while your right knee and left foot are in place, and if you deliberately threw yourself into the tan, you would be unhurt, and the riding-school horse knows better than to tread on anything unusual which he may find in his way.

Now, Esmeralda, keep your mind—No, your saddle is not turning; it is well girthed. You feel as if it were? Pray, how do you know how you would feel if a saddle were to turn? Did you ever try it? And your saddle is not too large! Neither is it too small! And there is nothing at all the matter with your horse! Now, Esmeralda, keep your mind—No, that other girl is not going to ride you down. Her horse would not allow her, if she endeavored to do so. The trouble is that she does not guide her horse, but is worrying herself about staying on his back, when she should be thinking about making him turn sharp corners and go straight forward. Regard her as a warning, Esmeralda, and keep your mind—What is the matter with the reins? Apparently they are oiled, for they have slipped from under your thumbs, and your horse is wandering along with drooping head, looking as if training to play the part of the dead warrior's charger at a military funeral.

Shorten your reins now, carefully! Not quite so much, or your horse will think that you intend to begin to trot, and do not lean backward, or he will fancy that you wish him to back or stop. The poor thing has to guess at what a pupil wishes, and no wonder that he sometimes mistakes.

But, Esmeralda, keep your mind on those thumbs and hold them close to your forefingers. Driving will give no idea of the slipperiness of leather, but after your first riding lesson you will wonder why it is not used to floor roller-skating rinks. But remember that your reins are for your horse's support, not for yours; they are the telegraph wires along which you send dispatches to him, not parallel bars upon which your weight is to depend. Hitherto, you have not ridden an inch. Your horse has strolled about, and you have not dropped from his back, and that is not riding, but now you shall begin.

In a large ring, pupils are required to keep to the wall when walking, as this gives the horse a certain guide, but in small rings the rule is to keep to the wall when trotting, so as to improve every foot of pace, and to walk about six feet from the wall, not in a circle, but describing a rectangle. New pupils are always taught to turn to the right, and to make all their movements in that direction. Hold your thumbs firmly in place, and draw your right hand a very little upward and inward, touching your whip lightly to the horse's right side, and turning your face and leaning your body slightly to the right.

The instant that the corner is turned, drop your hand, keeping the thumb in place, square your shoulders, look straight between your horse's ears, and then allow your eyes to range upward as far as possible without losing sight of him altogether. No matter what is going on about you. Very likely, the criticizing mamma on the mounting-stand is scolding sharply about noting. Possibly, a dear little boy is fairly flying about the ring on a pony that seems to have cantered out of a fairy tale, and a marvelously graceful girl, whom you envy with your whole soul, is doing pirouettes in the centre of the ring.

All that is not your business. Your sole concern is to keep your body in position, and your mind fixed on making your horse obey you, doing nothing of his own will. Stop him now and then by leaning back, and drawing on the reins, not with your body but with your hands. Then lean forward and go on, but if he should remain planted as fast as the Great Pyramid, if when started he should refuse to pay any attention to the little taps of your left heel and the touches of your whip, nay, if he should lie down and pretend to die, like a trick horse in a circus, don't cluck. No good riding master will teach a pupil to cluck or will permit the practice to pass unreproved, and riding-school horses do not understand it, and are quite as likely to start at the cluck of a rider on the other side of the ring as they are when a similar noise is made by the person on their own backs.

But now, just as you have shortened your reins for the fortieth time or so, your master rides up beside you. You told him of your little three-lesson plan, and being wise in his generation, he smilingly assented to it. "Shall we trot?" he asks, in an agreeable voice. "Shorten your reins, now! Don't pull on them! Right shoulder back! Now rise from the saddle as I count, 'One, two, three, four!' Off we go!'" You would like to know what he meant by "off!" "Off," indeed! You thought you were "off" the saddle. You have been bounced up and down mercilessly, and have gasped, "Stop him!" before you have been twice around the ring, and not one corner have you been able to turn properly. As for your elbows, you know that they have been flying all abroad, but still—it was fun, and you would like to try again. You do try again, and you would like to try again. You do try again, and, at last, you are conscious of a sudden feeling of elasticity, of sympathy with your horse, of rising when he does, and then your master looks at you triumphantly, and says: "You rose that time," and leaves you to go to some other pupil. And then you walk your horse again, trying to keep in position, and you make furtive little essays at trotting by yourself, and find that you cannot keep your horse to the wall, although you pull your hardest at his left rein, the reason being that, unconsciously, you also pull at the right rein, and that he calmly obeys what the reins tell him and goes straight forward. Then your master offers to help you by lifting you, grasping your right arm with his left hand, and you make one or two more circuits of the ring, and then the hour is over and you dismount and go to the dressing-room.

Tired, Esmeralda? A little, and you do wonder whether you shall not be a bruised piece of humanity to-morrow. Not if your flesh be as hard as any girl's should be in these days of gymnasiums, but if you have managed to bruise a muscle or to strain one, lay a bottle of hot water against it when you go to bed and it will not be painful in the morning. If, in spite of warnings, you have been so careless about your underclothing as to cause a blister, a bit of muslin saturated with Vaseline, with a drop of tincture of benzoin rubbed into it, makes a plaster which will end the smart instantly.

This is not a physician's prescription, but is hat of a horseman who for years led the best riding class in Boston, and it is asserted that nobody was ever known to be dissatisfied with its effects. Muffle yourself warmly, Esmeralda, and hasten home, for nothing is easier than to catch cold after riding. Air your frock and cloak before an open fire to volatilize the slight ammoniacal scent which they must inevitably contract in the locker, and then be as good to yourself as the hostler will be to your poor horse. That is to say, give yourself a sponge bath in hot water, with a dash of Sarg's soap and almond meal in it, rubbing dry with a Turkish towel, and then dress and go down to dinner.

Looking at your glowing face and shining eyes, your father will tell your mother that she should have gone also, but when he marks the havoc which you make with the substantial part of the meal, and sees that your appetite for dessert is twice as good as usual, he will reflect upon his butcher's and grocer's bills, and, considering what they would be with provision to make for two such voracious creatures, he will say, "No, Esmeralda, don't take your mother!"

III.

Up into the saddle,
Lithe and light, vaulting she perched.
  *Hayne.*

And you still think, Esmeralda, that three lessons will be enough to make you a horse woman, and that by next Monday you will be able to join the road party, and witch the world with your accomplishments?

Very well, array yourself for conquest and come to the school. Talk is cheap, according to a proverb more common than elegant; but it is sinful to waste the cheapest of things. While you dress, you will meditate upon the sensation which it is your intention to make in the ring, and upon the humiliation which you will heap upon your riding master by showing wonderful ability to rise in the saddle. Although not quite ready to assert ability to ride hour after hour like a mounted policeman, you feel certain that you could ride as gracefully as he, and perhaps you are right, for official position does not confer wisdom in equitation. To say nothing of policemen, it is not many seasons since an ambitious member of the governor's staff presented himself before a riding master to "take a lesson, just to get used to it, you know; got to review some regiments at Framingham tomorrow." And when, after some trouble, he had been landed in the saddle, never a strap had he, and long before his lesson hour was finished, he was a spectacle to make a Prussian sentinel giggle while on duty.

And for your further encouragement, Esmeralda, know that it is but a few years ago that a riding master, in answer to a rebellious pupil who defended some sin against Baucher with, "Mr. —— of the governor's staff always does so," retorted, "There is just one man on the governor's staff who can ride, and I taught him; and if he had ridden like that !" An awful silence expressed so many painful possibilities that the pupil was meek and humble ever after, and yet it was not written in any newspaper that any of those ignorant colonels were thrown from their saddles in public, nor did the strapless gentleman furnish amusement to civilian or soldier by rolling on the grass at Framingham.

The truth is, that the number of persons able to judge of riding is smaller than the number able to ride, and that number is rather less than one in a hundred of those who appear on horseback either in the ring or on the road; but Boston could furnish a legion of men and women who find healthful enjoyment in the saddle, and who look passably well while doing it, and possibly you may add yourself to their ranks after a very few lessons, although there is—You are ready? Come then!

Into the saddle well thought, thanks to your master, but why that ghastly pause? Turn instantly, place your knee over the pommel and thrust your foot into the stirrup, if you possibly can, without waiting for assistance. Teachers of experience, riding masters, dancing masters, musicians, artists, gymnasts, will unite in telling you that unless a pupil's mental qualities be rather extraordinary, it is more difficult to impart knowledge at a second lesson than at the first, simply because the pupil gives less attention, expecting his muscles to work mechanically.

Undoubtedly, after long training, fingers will play scales, and flying feet whirl their owner about a ballroom without making him conscious of every muscular extension and contraction, but this facility comes only to those who, in the beginning, fix an undivided mind upon what they are doing, and who never fall into willful negligence.

Keep watch of yourself, manage yourself as assiduously as you watch and manage your horse, and ten times more assiduously than you would watch your fingers at the piano, or your feet in the dancing class, because you must watch for two, for your horse and for yourself. If you give him an incorrect signal, he will obey it, you will be unprepared for his next act, and in half a minute you will have a very pretty misunderstanding on your hands.

But there is no reason for being frightened. You cannot fall, and if your horse should show any signs of actual misbehavior, you would find your master at your right hand, with fingers of steel to grasp your reins, and a voice accustomed to command obedience from quadrupeds, howsoever little of it he may be able to obtain at first from well-meaning bipeds. You are perfectly safe with him, Esmeralda, not only because he knows how to ride, but because the strongest of all human motives, self-interest, is enlisted to promote your safety. "She said she was afraid to risk her neck," said an exhausted teacher, speaking the words of frankness to a spectator, as a timid and stupid pupil disappeared into the dressing-room, "and I told her that she could afford the risk better than I. If she broke it, than don't you know, it probably could not be mended, but mine might be broken in trying to save her, and, at the best, my reputation and my means of getting a livelihood would be gone forever in an instant. It's only a neck with her; it's life and wife and babies that I risk, and I'll insure her neck." And when the stupid pupil, who was a lady in spite of her dulness, came from the dressing-room, calmed and quieted, and began to offer a blushing apology, he repeated his remarks to her, and so excellent was the understanding established between them after this little incident that she actually came to be a tolerable rider. Feeling that he would tell her to do nothing dangerous to her, she was ready at his command to lie down on her horse's back and to raise herself again and again, and, after doing this a few times, and bending alternately to the right and to the left, the saddle seemed quite homelike, and to remain in it sitting upright was very easy for a few moments.

Only for a few moments, however, for the necessity of paying attention still remained, as it does with you, and again she stiffened herself, as you are doing now.

As Mr. Mead very justly says, in his "Horsemanship for Women," a lesson may be learned from a bag of grain set up on horseback, which is, that while the lower part of your body should settle itself almost lazily in place, the upper part, which is comparatively light, should sway slightly but easily with the horse's motion.

Manage to ride behind the girl who was teaching herself to do pirouettes the other day. Her horse is walking rapidly, and you could almost fancy that her prettily squared shoulders were part of him, so sympathetically do they respond to each step, but if you should let your horse straggle against hers and frighten him, you would see that no rock is more firmly seated then she.

If it should please your master to require you to perform the bending exercise, you will feel the advantage of having practiced it at home, for it is infinitely easier in the saddle than it is on the floor, and your riding master will be exceedingly pleased at the ease with which you effect it. There is no necessity for telling him that the little feat is quite familiar to you. The woman of sense keeps as many of her doings secret as she can, and the wise pupil confesses no knowledge except that derived from her master. Being, in spite of his superior knowledge, a mortal man, he will take twice the pains with her, and a hundredfold more pride in her if persuaded that she owes everything to him.

There is no reason to worry about a little stiffness during the first lessons. It is almost entirely nervousness, and will disappear as soon as you are quite comfortable and easy, but the beautiful flexibility of the good horsewoman comes only to her whose muscles are perfectly trained, and it is surprising how few muscles there are to which one may not give employment in an hour's practice in the ring. If you like, you may, without the assistance of your master, lean forward to the right side until your left shoulder touches your horse's crest, and when you are trotting it is well how and then to lean forward and to the right until you can see your horse's forefeet, but you would better not perform the same exercise on the left side for the present, for you might overbalance yourself and almost slip from the saddle. If able, as you should be, to touch the floor with your fingertips without bending your knees, this little movement will be nothing to you, but do *not* bend to the left, Esmeralda. Why not? Why, because if you will have the truth, you are slipping to the left already, your right shoulder is drooping forward, and your weight is hanging in your stirrup and pulling your saddle to the left so forcibly that your horse has lost all respect for you, and would be thoroughly uncomfortable, were it not that you have forgotten all about your thumbs, and you have allowed your reins to slip away from you, so that he is going where he pleases, except when you jerk him sharply to the right, and then he shakes and tosses his head and goes on contentedly, as one saying, "All things have an end, even a new pupil's hour."

Now, sit well to the right, remembering the meal sack; shorten your reins, keeping your elbows down and your hands low. Shorten them a very little more, so as to bring your elbows further forward. When you stop, you should not be compelled to jerk your elbows back of your waist, but should bring them into line with it, leaning back slightly, and drawing yourself upward. Stop your horse now, for practice. Do not speak to him during your first lessons, except by your master's express command, but address him in his own language, using your reins, your foot, and your whip, if your master permit. "Why do you make coquette of your horse?" asked a French master of a pretty girl who was coaxingly calling her mount "a naughty, horrid thing," and casting glances fit to distract a man on the ungrateful creature's irresponsive crest. "Your horse does not care anything at all about you; don't you think he does!" pursued he, ungallantly. "You may coax me as much as you like," said a Yankee teacher to a young woman who was trying the "treat him kindly" theory, and was calling her horse a "dear old ducky darling;" "and," he continued, "I'm rather fond of candy myself, but it isn't coaxing or lump sugar that will make that horse go. It's brains and reins and foot and whip."

When you have a horse of your own, talk to him as much as you like, and teach him your language as an accomplishment, but address the riding-school horse in his own tongue, until you have mastered it yourself.

Now, adjust yourself carefully, lean forward, extend your hands a very little, touch your horse with your left heel, and, as soon as he moves, sit erect and let your hands resume their position. Hasten his steps until he is almost trotting, before you strike him with the whip. You can do this by very slightly opening and shutting your fingers in time with the slight pull which he gives with his head at every step, by touches with your heel, and by touches, not blows, with the whip, and by allowing yourself, not to rise, but to sit a little lighter with each step. It is not very easy to do, and you need not be discouraged if you cannot effect it after many trials. Some masters will tell you to strike your horse on the shoulder, and some will prefer that you should strike him on the flank as a signal for trotting. Those who prefer the former will tell you to carry your whip pointing forward; the others will tell you to carry it pointing backward, and many masters will say that it makes little difference as long as it is carried gracefully, and as long as you understand that it takes the place of a leg on the right side of the horse. General Anderson, in "On Horseback," lays down the rule that a horse should never be struck on the shoulder, as it will cause him to swerve, but use your master's horses in obedience to his orders.

Now, then, one, two, three, four! One, two, three, four! You don't seem to be astonishing anybody very much, Esmeralda! Again, one, two, three, four! Never mind! Sit down and let the horse do the work. Keep your left heel down, and your left knee close to the saddle. Not close to the pommel, understand, but close to the saddle. Try and imagine, if you like, that you are carrying a dollar between the knee and the saddle, after the West Point fashion, and do not fret overmuch because you are not rising. If you were a cavalryman riding with your troop, you would not be allowed to rise, and to sit properly while sitting close is an accomplishment not to be despised. "Ow!" What does that mean? You rose without trying? Watch yourself carefully, and if such a phenomenon should occur again, try to make it repeat itself by letting yourself down into the saddle, and then rising again quickly. But keep trotting! Count how many times you trot around the ring, and mentally pledge yourself to increase the number of circuits at your next lesson. And—"Cluck!"

Sit down in the saddle, Esmeralda! Lean back a little, bring your left knee up against the pommel, keeping the lower part of the leg close against the saddle; keep your right knee in place and your right foot and the lower part of your right leg close to the saddled; guide your horse, but do not otherwise exert yourself. How do you like it?

Delightful? Yes, with a good horse it is as delightful as sitting in a rocking-chair, but, if you were a rider of experience, you would not allow your horse to enter upon the gait without permission, but would bring him back to the trot by slightly pulling first the left rein and then the right, a movement which is called sawing the mouth. The poor creature is really not in fault. He heard the cluck given by that complacent-looking man, trotting slowly about, and not knowing how to use his reins and knees in order to go faster, and he said to himself: "She is tired of trotting and wants a rest; so do I," and away he went. If you had been trying to rise, you might have been thrown, for the greatest danger that you will encounter in the school comes from rising while the horse is at a canter. The cadence of the motion is triple, instead of in common time like that of the trot, and you will soon distinguish the difference, but eschew cantering at first. If you once become addicted to it, you will never learn to trot, or even to walk well.

Having had your little warning against clucking, perhaps you will now sympathize with the indignant Englishwoman who, having been almost unseated by a similar mischance, responded, when the clucking cause thereof rode up to say that he was sorry that her horse should behave so: "It wasn't the horse that was in fault, sir; it was a donkey." But now, try a round or two more of trotting, then guide your horse carefully about the ring two or three times, bring him up to the mounting-stand, dismount, and go to the dressing-room. You are rather warm, but not in the least tired, and you have had "such a good time," as you enthusiastically explain to everybody who will listen to you, but as there is much merry chatter going on from behind screens, and as it is all to the same effect, nobody pays much attention, and if you were cross and complaining, everybody would laugh at you. A riding-school is a place from which every woman issues better contented than she entered, and there is no sympathy for grumblers.

Remember to be careful about your wraps, and that you may be able to ride better next time, practice these exercises at home: Place your knees together and heels together, adjust your shoulders, hands, and arms as if you were in the saddle, and sit down as far as possible, while keeping the legs vertical from the knee down. Rise, counting "One," sink again, rise once more at "Two," and continue through three measures, common time. Rest a minute and repeat until you are a little weary. Nothing is gained by doing too much work, but if you do just enough of this between lessons, you cannot possibly grow stiff. When you can do it fairly well, try to do it first on one foot and then on the other, and then bring your right foot in front of your left knee, and, standing on your left foot, assume, as nearly as possibly, the proper position for the saddle, and try to rise in time. You will not find it very difficult, and you will be compelled to keep your heel down while doing it, especially if you put a block about an inch thick under your left tow. You may try doing it while sitting sidewise in a chair, if it be difficult for you to poise yourself on one foot, but a girl who cannot stand thus for some time, long enough to lace her riding boot, for instance, is much too weak for her own good.

Take all your spare minutes for this work, Esmeralda. Bob up and down in all the secluded corners of the house; try to feel the motion in the horse-cars—it will not need much effort in many of them. And if you want to be comfortable in a herdic, sit sidewise and pretend that the seat is a horse. This is Mr. Hurlburt's rule for riding in an Irish "outside car." In short, while taking your first riding-lessons, walk, sit, and think to the tune of

"One, two, three, four!
  Near the wall,
Make him trot;
  You cannot fall!"

IV.

The Horse does not attempt to fly;
He knows his powers, and so should I.
*Spurgeon.*

Wilful will to water, eh, Esmeralda? You are determined to appear in that riding party after your third lesson, and you think that you "will look no worse than a great many others." Undoubtedly, that is true, and more's the pity, but, since you will go, let us make the most of the third lesson, and trust that you will return in a whole piece, like Henry Clay's pie.

You do not see why there is any more danger on the road than in the ring, and you have never been thrown! It would be unkind, in the face of that "never," to remind you that you have been in the saddle precisely twice, and, really, there is no more danger from your incompetency, should it manifest itself on the road, than might arise from its display in the ring, but with your horse it is another matter. Having the whole world before him, why not, he will meditate, speed forth into space, and escape from the hateful creature who jerks on his head so causelessly, making him sigh wearily for the days of his unbroken colthood? He would endure it within doors, because he has noticed that his tormentor gives place to another every hour, and pain may be borne when it is not monotonous; but he remembers that there is no limit to the time during which one human being may impel him along an open road, and he also remembers some very pretty friskings, delightful to himself, but disconcerting to his rider, and he may perform some of them.

Even if he should, he would not unseat a rider well accustomed to school work, but you! You actually rose in the saddle three times in succession, the other day, and where were your elbows and where were your feet when you ceased rising, and long before your steady, quiet mount understood that you desired him to walk?

Your master smiles indulgently when you announce that this is your last practice lesson, and says: "Very well, you shall ride Charlie, to-day, at least for a little while, until some others come in." He himself mounts, moves off a pace or two, one of the assistant masters puts you in the saddle, and before the groom lets Master Charlie's head go, your master says, easily: "Leave his reins pretty long, especially the right one. Put your left knee close against the pommel; don't try to rise until I tell you. Ready. Now."

You feel as if you were in a transformation scene at the theatre. The windows of the ring seem to run into one another, and at very short intervals you catch a glimpse in the mirror of a young woman, in a familiar looking Norfolk jacket, sitting with her elbows as far behind her as if held there by the Austrian plan of running a broomstick in front of the arms and behind the waist.

On and on! You earnestly wish to stop, but are ashamed to say so. Close at your right hand, pace for pace with you, rides your master, keeping up an unbroken fire of brief ejaculation: "Hands a little lower! Arms close to the side!" Shoulders square! Square! Draw your right shoulder backward and upward! Now down with your right elbow! Don't pull o the right rein! Don't lift your hands! You'll make him go faster!"

"I like this kind of trot," you say sweetly. "It's easier than the other kind."

"It isn't a trot; it's a canter," says your master, with a suspicion of dryness in his voice, "but you may make him trot if you like. Shorten both reins, especially the left. Whoa, Charlie! Wait until I say 'Now,' before you do it! Shorten both reins, especially the left; that will keep him to the wall, Then extend your left arm a little, and draw back your right; draw back your left and extend your right, and repeat until he comes down to a trot. That saws his mouth, and gives him something besides scampering to occupy his mind. Now we will start up again at a canter. Lengthen your reins, but remember to shorten them when you want to trot."

"Shall I tell you before hand, so that you may have time to make your horse trot, too?" you ask.

Esmeralda, you must have been reading one of those sweet books on etiquette which advise the horsewoman to be considerate of her companions. How much notice do you think your master requires to "make his horse trot"? You will blush over the memory of that question next year, although now you feel that you have been very ladylike, even very Christian, in putting it, for have you not shown that your temper is unruffled and that you are thinking how to make others happy?

Your master answers that his horse may be trusted, and that if you prefer to take your own time to change from the canter to the trot, rather than to wait for him to say, "Now," you may do so. And the canter begins again, and, after a round or two, you try the mouth-sawing process, doing it very well, for it is an ugly little trick at best, rarely found necessary by an accomplished rider, and beginners seldom fail to succeed in it at the very first attempt. If it were pretty and graceful, it would be more difficult. Down to the trot comes the obedient Charles, and up you go one, two, three, four! And down you come, until you really expect to find yourself and the saddle in the tan between the two halves of your horse.

Of what can the creature's spinal column be made, to bear such a succession of blows! You begin by pitying the horse, but after about half a circuit, you think that human beings have their little troubles also, and you feel a suspicion of sarcasm in your master's gentle: "You need not do French trot any longer, unless you like. It will be easier for you to rise."

You give a frantic hop in your stirrup at the wrong minute, and begin a series of jumps in which you and the horse rise on alternate beats, by which means your saddle receives twice as much pounding as at first, and then you have breath enough left to gasp "Stop," and in a second you are walking along quietly, and your master is saying in a matter-of-fact way: "You would better keep your left heel down all the time, and turn the toe toward the horse's side and keep your right foot and leg close to the saddle below the knee; swing yourself up and down as a man does; don't drop like a lump of lead."

"Like a snowflake," you murmur, for you fancy that you have a pretty wit like Will Honeycomb.

"Not at all," says your master. "The snowflake comes down because it must, and comes to stay. You come because you choose, and come down to rise again instantly. You must keep your right shoulder back, and your hands on a level with your elbows, and you must turn the corners, not let your horse turn them as he pleases—but more pupils are coming now and I must give you another horse. You may have Billy Buttons." The change is effected, the other pupils begin their lessons, and you and Billy walk deliberately about in the centre of the ring.

At first he keeps moderately near the wall, but after a time you find that the circle described by his footsteps has grown smaller, and that he apparently fancies himself walking around a rather small tree. Your master rides up as you are pulling and jerking your left rein in the endeavor to come nearer to the wall, and says, "Try Billy's canter. I'll take a round with you. Strike him on the shoulder, and when you want him to trot, shorten your reins and touch him on the flank. Those are the signals which he minds best. Now! Canter."

You remember having heard of a "canter like a rocking-chair." Charlie had it, but you were too inexperienced to know it, but bad riders long ago deprived Billy of any likeness to a rocking-chair. He knows that if he should let himself go freely, you would come near to making him rear by pulling on the reins, and so he goes along "one, two, three, one, two, three," deliberately, and you feel and look, as you hear an unsympathetic gazer in the gallery remark, "like a pea in a hot skillet." You prided yourself on keeping your temper unruffled under the wise criticism of your master, but in truth you did not really believe him. You said to yourself that he was too particular, and you even thought of informing him that he must not expect perfection immediately, but this piece of impudence, spoken by a person who, for aught that you can tell, does not know Billy from a clotheshorse, convinces you instantly, and you decide to canter no more, but to trot, and so you "shorten your reins and strike him on the flank."

As you shorten the right rein more than the left, and as your whip falls as lightly as if you meant the blow for yourself, Billy goes to the centre of the ring, but you jerk him to the wall, and in time, trot he does. But your left foot swings now forward and now outward, and you cannot rise. The regular, pulsating count by which a clever girl is moving like a machine, irritates you, and you tell another beginner, "They really ought to let us rise on alternate bats at first, until we are more accustomed to the motion," and she agrees with you, and both of you try this, which might be called trotting on the American pupil plan, but even the calm Billy manages to take about six steps between what you regard as the "alternate beats," and at last breaks into a canter, and you hear yourself ordered, very peremptorily, to "sit down." You obey, but begin the pea in the skillet performance again, and at last you tell your master that you will not try to trot anymore, but would like to know all about managing the reins.

"And then," you say, looking as wise as the three Gothamites of the nursery song, "even if I should not be able to trot long, and should fall behind my friends on the road, I shall have perfect control of my horse, and can walk on until they miss me and turn back for me. Will you please tell me all the ways of holding the reins?"

Your master does not laugh; the joke is too venerable, and he feels awe-struck as he hears it, so ancient does it seem.

"If you take your reins in one hand," he says, "an easy way is to hold the snaffle on your ring finger, and the left curb outside the little finger, with the right curb between the middle and fore fingers. Then, when you want to use both hands, put your right little finger and ring finger between the right curb and right snaffle, and hold your hands at exactly even distances from your horse's head, with the two reins firmly nipped by the thumbs resting on top of the fore-fingers. This is the way recommended in the Encyclopaedia

Britannica, in Colonel Dodge's 'Patroclus and Penelope,' and you will see it in many very good hunting pictures.

"Colonel Anderson, in his 'On Horseback,' recommends dividing the curb reins by the little finger of the left hand and the snaffle reins by the middle finger, carrying the ends up through the hand, and holding them by the thumb. Mr. Mead, in his 'Horsemanship for Women,' mentions this hold, but prefers taking the curb on the ring finger, and the snaffle outside the little finger, and between the forefinger and middle finger. This hold is used in the British army, and it is convenient in school, because if it be desirable to drop the curb in order to ride with the snaffle only, you can do it by dropping your ring finger, and, if your horse be moderately quiet, you can knot the curb rein and let it lie on his neck. Besides, it makes the snaffle a little tighter than the curb, and that is held to be a good thing in England. An English soldier is prone to accuse American cavalrymen of riding too much on the curb, and by the way, I have heard English soldiers assert that they were taught the second method, but it was a riding master formerly in the Queen's service who told me that the third was preferred.

"M. de Bussigny, in his little 'Handbook for Horsewomen,' gives the preference to crossing the reins, the curb coming outside the little finger and between the ring and middle finger, and the snaffle between the little and ring fingers and the middle finger and forefinger. I hold my won in that way when training a horse, but it is better for you to use both hands on the reins, and he would tell you so. You are more likely to sit square; it gives you twice the hold, and then, too, you know where your right hand is, and are not waving it about in the air, or devising queer ways of holding your whip. Now your hour is over, and I will take you off your horse. Wait until he is perfectly still, and the groom has him by the head. Now drop your reins; let me take off the foot straps; take your foot out of the stirrup; turn in the saddle; put one hand on my shoulder and one on my elbow, and slip down as lightly as you can."

You glance at the clock, perceive that you have been I the saddle almost an hour and a half, and murmur an apology. "Don't mind," is the encouraging answer. "As long as a pupil does not complain and call us stingy when we make her dismount, we do not say much. But are you really going on the road, Monday, Miss Esmeralda?" "Yes, I am," you answer. "Ah, well," he says, a little regretfully, "don't forget, then. Hold on with your right knee and sit down for the canter."

What shall you do by way of exercise before Monday? Practise all the old movements, a little of each one at a time, and take two lengths of ribbon as wide as an ordinary rein, or, better still, two leather straps, and fasten one to the knobs on the two sides of a door and run the other through the keyhole. Call the knob straps the snaffle reins, and the keyhole straps the curb, and, sitting near enough to let them lie in your lap, practice picking them up and adjusting them with your eyes shut. When you can do it quickly and neatly, try and see with how little exertion you can sway the door to left and right, and then practice holding these dummy reins while standing on one foot and executing the movement used in trotting. If the door move by a hair's breadth, it will show you that you are pulling too much, and you must remember that your hold on your horse's mouth gives you greater leverage than you have on the door, and then, perhaps, you will pity the poor beast a little now and then.

What is that? Your master treated you as if you were an ignorant girl? So you are, dear, and even if you were not, if you knew all that there is in all the books, you might still be a bad horsewoman, because you might now know enough to use your knowledge. You don't care, and you feel very well, and are very glad that you went? Of course, that is the invariable cry! And you mean to take some more lessons if you find that you really need them? Then leave your skirt in the dressing-room locker! You will come back from your ride a wiser, but not a sadder, girl. One cannot be sad on horseback.

## V.

—Pad, pad, pad! Like a thing that was mad,
　My chestnut broke away.
　　*Thornbury.*

Esmeralda was puzzled when she returned from her first riding party. In the morning, looking very pretty in her borrowed riding habit, her English hat with the hunting guard made necessary by the Back Bay breezes, her brown gauntlets, and the one scarlet carnation in her button-hole, she drove to the riding-school, where she had agreed to meet Theodore and her other friends, not like Mrs. Gilpin, lest all should say that she was proud, but because her master had promised to lend her one of the school horses, to put her ion the saddle and to adjust her stirrup, and because she secretly felt that she would better give herself every possible advantage in what, as it came nearer, assumed the aspect of a trial rather than a pleasure.

Beholding Ronald, the promised horse, severely correct in his road saddle, and looking immensely tall as he stood on the stable floor, she inly applauded her own wisdom, strongly doubting that Theodore's unpractised arm would have tossed her into her place as lightly as the master's, and she was secretly overjoyed when the master himself mounted and joined the party with her, making its number nine; Esmeralda herself, the graduate of three lessons; Theodore, all his life accustomed to ride anything calling itself a horse, but making no pretenses to mastery of the equestrian science; the lawyer, understood, on his own authority, to be well informed in everything; the society young lady, erect, precise, self-satisfied; the Texan, riding with apparent laziness, his hands rather high and seldom quiet, but not to be shaken from his seat; the beauty, languid and secretly discontented because her horse was "intended for a brunette, and a ridiculous mount for a blonde"; Versatilia, who had "taken up riding a little," and the cavalryman, calm, quiet, and fraternally regarded by the master, as he reviewed the little flock from the back of a horse which had been offered to him as the paragon of its species, and for which and its kind, as he announced after riding a square or two, he "was not paying a cent a carload."

"It is a lovely horse," said the beauty. "It is such a beautiful color. But men never care for color."

"Good color is a good thing, undoubtedly," said the master, "but a beautiful horse is a good horse, not necessarily an animal which would look well in a painted landscape, because its color would harmonize with the hue of the trees."

"She is a beautiful girl, isn't she," said Esmeralda, looking admiringly at the beauty, who, having just remembered Tennyson's line about swaying the rein with flying finger tips, was executing some movements which made her horse raise his ears to listen for the cause of such conduct, and then shake his head in mild disapproval.

"What do I care for a pretty girl?" demanded the master. "Pretty rider is what I want to see, and 'pretty rider' is 'good rider.' Wait until that girl trots three minutes or so, and see whether or not she is pretty."

The party went through the streets at a rapid walk, now and then meeting a horse-car, now and then a stray wagon, but invariably allowed to take its own way, with very little regard for the rule of the road. The American who drives, whatever may be his social station, admires the courage of the woman who rides, but he is firmly convinced that she does not understand horses, and gives her all the space available wherein to disport herself.

"Are we all right in placing the ladies on the left?" asked Theodore, turning to the master.

"Of course," cried the lawyer. "We follow the English rule, and the left was the place of safety for the lady in the days when English equestrianism was born. Travelers took the left of the road, and this placed the cavalier between his lady and any possible danger."

"And in the United States they take the right, and she is between him and any possible danger," said the master. "It is the custom, but it seems illogical and foolish. True, it removes any danger that the lady may be crushed between her own horse and her escort's, but who protects her from any passing car or carriage, and in case of a runaway what can her escort, his left hand occupied with his own reins, do to aid her with hers, or to disentangle her foot from the stirrup or her habit from the pommels in case she is thrown? Can he snatch her from the saddle, after the matter of one of Joaquin Miller's young men? The truth is that since the rule of the road is 'keep to the right,' the rule of the saddle should be 'sit on the right,' but with a lady on his bridle hand the horseman could not be at his best as an escort, even then.

"It is one of the many little absurdities in American customs; the old story of the survival of the two buttons at the back of the coat, and, by the way, Miss Esmeralda, the two buttons on the back of your habit are out of place, not because of your tailor's fault, but because of yours. They should make a line at right angles with your horse's spinal column. Draw yourself back a little, until you can feel the pommel under your right knee. 'Draw' yourself back; don't lean, but keep yourself perfectly erect, your back perpendicular to your horse's. Sit a little to the left; lean a little to the right. Let your left shoulder go forward a little, your right shoulder backward. Now you are exactly right. Try to remember your sensations at this minute, in order to be able to reproduce them. When I say 'Careful,' pass yourself in review and endeavor to feel where you are wrong. But," addressing the cavalryman, who was in advance with Versatilia, "is this procession a funeral?"

"Not exactly," said the cavalryman, and the, after a backward glance, he cried, in the fashion of a military riding-school master: "Pr-r-re-pare to tr-r-r-ot—Trot!"

Esmeralda remembered to shorten her reins, and resigned herself to the Fates, who were propitious, enabling her to catch the cadence of the trot, and to rise to it during the few seconds before the cavalryman slackened rein. "Careful," said the master, and she shook herself into place, eliciting a hearty "Good!" from him. "Look at your pretty girl," he growled softly, but savagely, and truly the beauty solicited attention. Slipping to the left in her saddle, one elbow pointing toward Cambridgeport and the other toward Dorchester, her right foot visible through her habit, and her left all but out of the stirrup, she was attractive no longer, and to complete the master's disgust she ejaculated: "My hair is coming down!"

"Better bring a nurse and a ladies' maid for her," he muttered to Esmeralda, confidentially. "Hairpins in your saddle pocket? Well, you are a sensible girl," and he rode forward with the little packet, giving it to the lawyer to pass to the unfortunate young woman. But here arose a little difficulty. The space between the lawyer's horse and the beauty's as they stood was too wide to allow him to lay the parcel in her outstretched fingers. The Texan, on her right hand, had enough to do to keep her horse and his own absolutely motionless that she might not be thrown by any unexpected motion of either animal. Versatilia exclaimed in remonstrance, "Don't leave me," when the cavalryman said, "Wait a second, I'll come and give them to her;" the master sat quiet and smiling.

"Why don't you dismount and give them to her?" cried Theodore, and was out of his saddle, had placed the parcel in her hand, and was back in his place again before either of the other three men could speak.

"Very well done," said the master, approvingly, "but not the right thing to do. Never leave your saddle without good cause, and never leave your horse loose for a moment. Yes, I saw that you retained your hold of the reins; I was talking at Miss Esmeralda."

"Why didn't you make your horse step sideways?" he asked the lawyer.

"I can't. He won't. See there!"

Sundry pulls, precisely like those which he might have used had he intended the horse to turn, a pair of absolutely motionless legs, and an unused whip were accepted as evidence that the lawyer's "I can't" was perfectly true, and the master and the cavalryman exchanged comprehending glances as the latter said: "Well, don't mind. An eminent authority announced after the Boston horse show of 1889 that high-school airs were of no use on the road. To make a horse move a step sideways is the veriest little zephyr of an air, but it would have been of some use to you, then. Are we ready now? What's that? Dropped your whip?"

Up went the Texan's left heel, catching cleverly on the saddle as he dropped lightly to the right, after the fashion of the Arab, the Moor, the Apache, of all the nations which ride for speed and for fighting rather than for leaping and hunting, and he caught the whip from the ground and was back in his place in a twinkling. The ladies were unmoved, because inappreciative; the lawyer looked savagely envious, the cavalryman and the master approving, and Theodore, frankly admiring, but no one said anything, the little cavalcade rearranged itself, and once more moved on at a footpace until an electric car appeared.

"Ronald is like a rock," said the master, "and you need not be afraid, but I'll take this beast along in advance. He will shy, or do some outrageous thing, and he has a mouth as sensitive as the Mississippi's, and no more."

The "beast" did indeed sidle and fret and prance, and manifest a disposition to hasten to drown himself in the reservoir, beyond the reach of self-propelling vehicles, and he repeated the performance a the sight of two other cars, although evidently less alarmed than at first, but the fourth car was in charge of a kindly-disposed driver, who came to a dead stop, out of pure amiability.

This was too much for the "beast" to endure; a moving house he was beginning to regard as tolerable, but a house which stopped short and glared at him with all its windows was more than horse nature could endure, and he started for the next county to institute an inquiry as to whether such actions were to be allowed, but found himself forced to stop, and not altogether comfortable, while the master cried good-naturedly: "Go along and take care of your car. I'll take care of my horse!"

"More than some other folks can do," said the driver, with a quiet grin at the lawyer, whose angry, "Here, what are you doing!" shouted to his plunging steed, had brought all the women in the car to the front, to explain to one another that "that man was abusing his horse, poor thing."

The car glided off, and Versatilia turned to look at it; her horse stumbled slightly, jerking her wrists sharply, and but for the cavalryman's quick shifting of the reins to his right hand and his strong grasp of her reins with his left, she might have been in danger.

"Never look back," lectured the master. Esmeralda was his pupil, and he would have taken the whole centennial quadrille and all the cabinet ladies to point his moral, had he seen them making equestrian blunders. "Where your horse has been, where, he is, is the past. Look to the future, straight before you."

"The cavalryman looked back just now," Esmeralda ventured to say.

"Yes, but he turned his horse very slightly to do it, and he may do almost anything because he has a perfect seat, and is a good horseman."

"Suppose I hear something or somebody coming up behind me?"

"If it have any intelligence, it will not hurt you. If it have none, looking will do you no good. Turn out to the right as far as you can and look to the front harder than ever, so as to be ready to guide your horse and to avoid any obstacles in case he should start to run. What is the trouble with the ladies now?"

"O, dear!" cried the beauty to the society young lady, "your horse."

"What's the matter with him?" asked the other, still very stately and not turning.

"Oh! The dreadful creature has caught his tail on my horse's bit," said the beauty.

"Then you'd better take your horse's bit away," retorted the other. "My horse's eyes are not at that end of him, and he can't be expected to look at his tail."

"And you may be kicked," added the Texan. "Check him a little; there! We ought not to be so close together, and we ought to be moving a little, I think. Shall we trot again?"

Everybody assented, the cavalryman and Versatilia set off, the others followed as best they might, the beauty "going to pieces" in a minute or two, according to the master, the society young lady stiffening visibly, losing the cadence of the trot very soon, but making no outcry as she was tossed about uncomfortably, and not bending her head to look at her reins, as Versatilia did.

"There's the advantage of training in other things," said the master. "She's a good dancer and a good amateur actress, and she is controlling herself as she would on a ballroom floor, and remembering the spectators as she would on the stage. She's no rider, but is perfectly selfish and self-possessed, and she will cheat her escort into thinking that she is one. Glad she's no pupil of mine, however! She always heads the conversation, one of her friends told me the other day. That is to say, she is always acting. I can't teach such a person anything; nobody can. She can teach herself, as she can think of herself and love herself, but she can't go outside of herself — and the lawyer will find it out after he has married her."

Esmeralda and Theodore stared in astonishment.

"Walk," said the master, noticing that his pupil looked too warm for comfort, and the three allowed the others to go on without them. "Careful," he added, and Esmeralda, adjusting herself studiously, asked: "Is it really easier to ride on the road than it is in the school? It seems so."

"It is a little, especially if the corners of the ring are so near together that the horse goes in a circle, for then the rider has to lean to the right, while on the road she may sit straight. Give me the right kind of horse for my pupil to ride, and I would as leif give lessons on the road as anywhere, but it is not well for the pupil, whose attention is distracted by a thousand things, and who learns less in a year than she would in a month in school. There is no finish about the riding of a woman so taught. She may be pretty, as you said of one of your friends, she may be self-possessed, like the other, but she will betray her ignorance every moment. You were surprised just now at what I said of the society young lady. A woman can't cheat an old riding-master, after he has seen her in the saddle. He knows her and her little ways by heart. Shall we start up? Ah!"

Ronald, the "steady as a rock," was off and away at a canter; Theodore was starting to gallop in pursuit, but was sharply ordered back by the master, who went on himself at a rather slow canter, ready to break into a gallop if his pupil were thrown, but keeping out of Ronald's hearing, lest he should be further startled by finding himself followed. There was a clear stretch of road before her, and Esmeralda sat down as firmly as possible, brought her left knee up against the pommel, clung firmly with her right knee, held her hands low and her thumbs as firm as possible, and thought very hard.

"Very soon," she said to herself, "I shall be thrown and dragged, and hat a figure I shall be going home, if I', not killed! But I sha'n't be! I shall be ridiculous, and that's worse." Here she swept by the riding party, but as Versatilia and the beauty turned to look at her, and forgot to control their horses, the cavalryman and the Texan had to do it for them, and could do nothing for Esmeralda except to shout "Whoa," which Ronald very properly disregarded. The master came up, and the society young lady addressed him with, "Very silly of her to try to exhibit herself so, isn't it?"

"That's no exhibition; that's a runaway," said the master grimly. "She's doing well too, poor girl," and he and Theodore went on after the flying rider. Two or three carriages, the riders staring with horror; a pedestrian or two, innocently wondering why a lady should be on the road alone; a small boy whistling shrilly; these were all the spectators of Esmeralda's flight. She felt desolate and deserted, and yet sure that it was best that she should be alone, since the master could overtake her if he would, and she wondered if she should be very seriously injured when thrown at last, but all the time she was talking to Ronald in a voice carefully kept at a low pitch, and her hands were held with a steadiness utterly new to them, and the good horse went on regularly, but faster and faster.

"That isn't a real runaway," said the master to himself. "Ah, I see! Her whip is down and strikes him at every stride, and so she unconsciously urges him forward. If there were a side road here, I'd gallop around and meet her, or if there were fields on either side, I'd leap the fence and make a circuit and cut her off, but through this place, with banks like a railway cutting on each side, there is nothing to do."

Swifter and swifter! Esmeralda began to feel weaker, thought of Theodore, and of some other things of which she never told even him, said a little prayer, but all the time remembered her master's injunctions, and kept her place firmly, waiting for the final, and, as she believed, inevitable crash, when lo! She saw that just in front of her lay a long piece of half-mended road, full of ugly little stones, and she turned Ronald on it, with a triumphant, "See how you like that, sir," and then sawed his mouth. In half a minute he was walking. In another the master was beside her with words of approval. Theodore galloped up, pale and anxious, and between the two she had quite as much praise as was good for her, and, being told of the position of the whip, found her confidence in Ronald restored.

"But you should never start up hastily," said the master. "Take time for everything, and check your horse the instant he goes faster than you mean to have him. You are a good girl, and you shall not be scolded, or snubbed, either," he muttered, and the party came up, the cavalryman and the Texan loud in praise, the other four clamorous with questions and advice.

"You look quite disheveled," said the society young lady agreeably.

"Ladies often do after they have been on the road a little while. Excuse me, but one of your skirt buttons is unfastened," said the master, and, not knowing how to pass her reins into her right hand so as to use her left to repair the accident, the society young lady was effectually silenced, while the master, holding Esmeralda's horse, made her wipe her face, arrange the curly locks flying about her ears, readjust her hat, and generally smooth her plumage, until she was once more comfortable.

After a little, the master proposed a trot up the hill, and instructed Esmeralda to lean forward as her horse climbed upward, "If you should have to trot down hill, lean back a little, and keep your reins short," he said.

The lawyer and the society young lady, essaying to descend the next hill brilliantly, barely escaped going over their horses' heads, and all four ladies were glad when they perceived that they were going homeward.

"I like it," Esmeralda said to the master, "but I wish I knew more, and I'm going to learn, and I see now that three lessons isn't enough, even for a beginning."

"I knew a girl who took seventeen lessons and then was thrown," said the society young lady. "Native ability is better than teaching. I don't believe any master could make a rider of you, Esmeralda."

"A good teacher can make a rider out of anyone who will study," said the master, to whom she looked for approval. "As for seventeen lessons, they are better than seven, of course, but they are not much, after all. How many dancing lessons, music lessons, elocution lessons have you taken? More than seventeen? I thought so. Here's a railroad bridge, but no train coming. Had one been approaching, and had there been no chance to cross it before it came, I should have made you turn Ronald the other way, Miss Esmeralda, so that if he ran he would run out of what he thinks is danger, and not into it. And now for an easy little trot home."

An easy little trot it was, and Esmeralda, left at her own door, where a groom waited to take her horse to the stable, was happy, but puzzled. "Theodore," she cried, as soon as he appeared in the evening, "did you ask the master to go with us? He treated me just as he does in school."

"Yes, I did," said Theodore boldly. "I was afraid to take charge of you alone. That was a 'road lesson.'"

"You—you—exasperating thing!" cried Esmeralda. "But then, you were sensible."

"That's tautology," said Theodore.

VI.

A solitary horseman might have been seen.
*G.P.R. James.*

And so you are feeling very meek after your road lesson and your runaway, Esmeralda, and are a perfect Uriah Heep for 'umbleness, and are, henceforth and forever, going to believe every syllable that your master utters, and to obey every command the instant that it is given, and—there, that will do! And you are going to take one private lesson so as to learn a few little things before you display your progress before any other pupils again? One private lesson! Did your master advise it? No-no, but he consented to give it, when you had persuaded him that it would be best for you? When you had persuaded him? Behold the American pupil's definition of obedience: to follow commands dictated by herself! However, there is no use in trying to eradicate the ideas bequeathed and fostered by a hundred years of national self-government, so go to the school at the hour when no other pupils are expected.

The horses pace very solemnly around the great ring, and you adjust yourself with wonderful dignity, feeling that your master must perceive by your improved carriage and by the general perfection of your aspect that your exquisite timidity and charming shyness have been responsible for your awkwardness in former lessons, when other pupils were present, but now he leaves your side and takes a position in the centre of the ring, whence he addresses you thus:

"Keep your reins even! The right ones are too short, the left too long! Stop him! That is not stopping him! He took two steps forward after he checked himself. Go forward, and try again when I tell you. Stop! Not so hard, not so hard! You are making him back! Extend your arms forward! There! A little more, and you would have made him rear! Whoa! Wo-ho! Now listen! Not so! Don't drop your reins in that way, and sit so carelessly that a start would throw you from your place! Never leave your horse to himself a second! Sit as well as you can, look between your horse's ears and listen! Always use some discretion in choosing your place to stop. Do not try to stop when turning a corner, even to avoid danger, but rather change your direction. In the ring, never stop on the track, unless in obedience to your masters order, but turn out into the centre, but when you have once told your horse to stop, make him do it, for his sake, as well as for your own, if you have to spend an hour in the effort. And it will be an hour well spent, so that you need not lose patient, and if you do lose it, do not allow your horse to perceive it.

"To stop, you should press your leg and your whip against your horse's sides; lift your hands a very little, and turn them in toward your body, lean back and draw yourself up. There are six things to do: two to your horse, one on each side of him, two with your hands and two with your body, and you must do them almost simultaneously. Unless you do the first two, your horse will surely take a forward step or two after stopping, in order to bring himself into a comfortable position. If you do not cease doing the last four the moment that your horse has stopped, he may rear or he may back several steps, and he should never do that, but should await an order for each step. Now, do you remember the six things? Very well! Go forward! Stop! Did I tell you to do anything with your arms? No> Well, why did you bring your elbows back of your waist, then? It is allowable to do that—to save your life, but not to stop your horse. Bend your hands at the wrist, turning the knuckles, if need be, until they are at right angles with their ordinary position, so that the back of your hand is toward your horse's ears, but keep the thumb uppermost all the time.

"Now, think it over a moment! Go forward! Stop! Pretty well! Go on! Don't lean forward too much when you start, and sit up again instantly.

"Now walk around the school once, and go into all the corners. Stop! You stopped pretty well, but you leaned back too far, and you did not draw yourself up at all. Mind, you draw 'yourself' up; you don't try to pull the bit up through the corners of your horse's mouth. What I wanted to say was that a turn is just half a stop as far as your hands, leg and whip are concerned. To turn to the right, use your right hand and whip, but keep your left leg and hand steady; to turn to the left, use your left leg and hand and keep your whip and whip hand steady. When you turn to the right, lean to the right instead of backward; 'lean,' not twist to the right, and turn your head to the right so as to see what may be there.

"If you were on the road, and did not turn your head before going down a side street, you might knock over a bicycle rider, and thereby hurt your horse, which would be a pity," he says, with apparent indifference as to the bicycle rider's possible injuries. "Now go around the school again. Left shoulder forward! Right shoulder back! Sit to the right! Lean to the left! I told you to sit to the left, the other day? And that is the reason that I have told you to sit to the right to-day. You over-do it. Miss Esmeralda, if I were talking for my own pleasure, I should say pretty things to you, but I am talking to teach you, and when I say 'This is wrong! This is wrong!' and again 'This is wrong!' I do it for you, not for myself. When your father and mother say 'This is wrong; you must not do it, or you will be sorry,' you do not look at them as if you thought them to be unreasonable — or, I trust that you do not," he adds, mentally. "Heaven only knows what an American girl may do when anybody says, 'You must not' to her.

"Now," he goes on aloud, "it is the same with your teacher; he says 'You are wrong,' lest you should be sorry by and by, and he is patient and says it many times, as your father and mother do, and he says it every time that you do anything wrong, unless you do so many wrong things at once that he cannot speak of each one. Now you shall turn to the right, and remember that a turn is half a stop. Go across the school and then turn to the left! Keep a firm hold on your right rein now so as to keep your horse close to the wall. Where, where are your toes? It was not necessary to make you turn so as to see your right foot through your riding habit as I can now, to know that they were pointing outward. Your right shoulder told the story by drooping forward. M. de Bussigny lays especial stress on this point in his manual, and you will find that your whole position depends more on that seemingly unimportant right foot than on many other things, so bend your will to holding it properly, close against the saddle. Walk on now, keeping on a straight line. If you cannot do it in the school, you cannot on the road, and many an ugly scrape against walls, horse-cars, and other horses you will receive unless you can keep to the right and in a straight line. Now turn to the left, and go straight across the school. Straight! Fix your eye on something when you start, and ride at it with as much determination as if it were a fence; now you turn to the right again and go forward. Have you read Delsarte?"

No, you murmur to yourself, you have not read Delsarte, and, if you had, you do not believe that you could remember it or anything else just at present. What an endless string of directions! You wish that there was another pupil with you to take the burden of a few of them! You wish you were—oh! Anywhere. This is your obedience, is it Esmeralda? Well, you don't care! This is dull! Your horse thinks so, too. He gently tries the reins, and, finding that you offer no resistance, he decides to take a little exercise, and starts off at a canter, keeping away from the wall most piously, avoiding the corners as if some Hector might be in ambuscade there to catch and tame him, and rushing on faster and faster, as you do nothing in particular to stop him.

"Lean to the right," cries the master, and you obey, but the horse continues his canter, almost a gallop now, when suddenly your wits return to you, you draw back first the right hand and then the left, he begins to trot, and by some miracle you begin to rise, and continue to do it, you do not know exactly how, feeling a delight in it, an exhilarating, exultant sensation as if flying. "Keep your right leg close to the saddle below the knee and turn your toes in!" You obey, and even remember to press your left knee to the saddle also and to keep your heel down. "Don't rise to the left! Rise straight! Your horse is circling to the right, and you must lean to the right to rise straight! Take him into the corners so that he will move more on a straight line, and you can rise straight and be as much at ease as if on the road. Whoa! Now, don't change your position, but look at yourself! You did not shorten your reins when you began to trot, and, if your horse had stumbled, you could not have aided him to regain his balance. Had you shortened them properly, you could, by sitting down, using your leg and whip lightly and turning your hands toward your body, have brought him down to a walk without hurling yourself forward against the pommel in that fashion. Now, adjust yourself and your reins, and start forward once more," and you obey, and are beginning to flatter yourself that your master does not know that your canter was accidental, when he warns you against allowing a horse to do anything unbidden.

"You should have stopped him at once," he says. "He will very likely try to repeat his little maneuver in a few minutes. When he does, check him instantly, not by your voice, but as you have been directed. And now, have you read Delsarte? No? If you have time, you might read a chapter or two with advantage, simply for the sake of learning that a principle underlies all attitudes.

"He divides the body into three parts; the head, torso, and legs, and he teaches that the first and third should act on the same line, while the second is in opposition to them. For instance, if you be standing and looking toward the right, your weight should rest on your right leg and your torso should be turned to the left. Neither turn should be exaggerated, but the two should be exactly proportioned, one to another.

"Now for riding, your body is divided into three parts, your head and torso making one, your legs above the knee, the second, and your legs below the knee, the third, and you will find that the first and third will act together, whether you desire it or not. Your right foot is properly placed now, but turn its toes outward and upward; you see what becomes of your right shoulder. Now try to make a circle to the right, a volte we call it, because it is best to become accustomed to a few French words, as there are really no English equivalents for many of the terms used in the art of equestrianism.

"To make a volte you have only to turn to the right and to keep turning, going steadily away from the wall until opposite your starting point, and then regaining it by a half-circle. Making voltes is not only a useful exercise, showing your horse that you really mean to guide him, and teaching you to execute a movement steadily, but

45

it affords an excellent way of diverting the horse's attention from the mischief which Satan is always ready to find for idle hoofs. Give him a few voltes and he forgets his plans for setting off at a canter. Do you understand? Very well. When you are half-way down the school try to make a volte. I will give you no order. Your horse would understand if I did and would begin the movement himself, and you should do it unaided."

You try the volte, and convince yourself that the geometry master who taught you that a circle was a polygon with an infinite number of sides was more exact and less poetical than you thought him in the days before the riding-school began to reform your judgment on many things. You are conscious of not making a respectable curve in return, and you draw a deep breath of disgust as you say, "That was very bad, wasn't it?"

"Not for the first time. Keep your left hand and leg steady, and try it again on the other side of the ring. Better! Now walk around, and make him go into the corners, if you have to double your left wrist in doing it, but don't move your arm, and when you begin to bend you right wrist to turn, straighten your left, and remember to lean your body and turn your head, if you want your horse to turn his body. Your wrist acts on his head and keeps him in line; your whip and leg bring his hind legs under him, but you must move your body if you want him to move his.

"Now, you shall make a half volte, or shall 'change hands,' as it is sometimes called, because, if you start with your left hand nearest the wall, you will come back to the wall with your right hand nearest to it; or, to speak properly, 'if you start on the right hand of the school, you will end on the left hand.' For the half volte, make a half circle to the right, and then ride in a diagonal line to a point some distance back on your track, and when you are close to it make three quarters of a turn to the left and you will find yourself on the left of the school, and in a position to practice keeping your horse to the right. Try it, beginning about two thirds of the way down the long side of the school. Now to get back to the right hand, you may turn to the left across the school, and turn to the left again.

"There is a better way of dong it, but that is enough for to-day. Walk now. Do you see how much better your horse carries himself, and how much better you carry your hands, after those little exercises? Now you must try and imagine yourself doing them over and over and over again, to accustom your mind to them, just as when learning to play scales and five-finger exercises you used to think them out while walking. Shall you not need pictures and diagrams to assist you? Not if you have as much imagination as any horsewoman should have. Not if you have enough imagination to manage a cow, much more to enter into the feelings of a good horse. Pictures are invaluable to the stupid; they benumb and enervate the clever, and turn them into apish imitators, instead of making them able to act from their own knowledge and volition. Theory will not make you a good rider, but a really good rider without theory is an impossibility, and your theory must have a deeper seat than your retinae. Now, you shall have a very little trot, and then you may walk for ten minutes, and try to do voltes and half voltes by yourself, asking me for aid if you cannot remember how to execute the movements. Doing them will help you to pass away the time when you are too tired to trot, and will keep you from having any dull moments."

And you, Esmeralda, you naughty girl! You forgot all about your sulkiness half an hour ago, and, looking your master in the face, you say: "But nobody ever has dull moments in riding-school." There! Finish your lesson and walk off to the dressing-room; you will be trying to trade horses with somebody the next thing, you artful, flattering puss!

VII.

Here we are riding, she and I!
*Browning.*

What is it now, Esmeralda? By your blushing and stammering it is fairly evident that another of your devices for learning on the American plan—that is to say, by not studying—is in full possession of your fancy, and that again you expect to become a horsewoman by a miracle; come, what is it? A music ride? Nell has an acquaintance who always rides to music, and asserts that it is as easy as dancing; that the music "fairly lifts you out of the saddle," and that the pleasure of equestrian exercise is doubled when it is done to the sound of the flute, violin, and bassoon, or whatever may be the riding-school substitutes?

As for lifting you out of the saddle, Esmeralda, it is quite possible that music might execute that feat, promptly and neatly, once, and might leave you out, were it produced suddenly and unexpectedly by "dot leetle Sherman bad," and it is undoubtedly true that, were you a rider, music would exhilarate you, quicken your motions, stimulate your nerves, and assist you as it assists a soldier when marching. It is also true that it will aid even you somewhat, by indicating on what step you should rise, so that your motions will not alternate with those of your horse, to your discomfiture and his disgust, and that thus, by mechanically executing the movement, you may acquire the power of seeing that you are not performing it when you rise once a minute or thereabouts, but a music ride is an exercise which a wise pupil will not take until advised thereto by her master. Still, have your own way! Why did George Washington and the other fathers of the republic exist, if its daughters must be in bondage to common sense and expediency?

Borrow Nell's habit once more, for the criticism to be undergone on the road is mild compared to that of a gallery of spectators before whom you must repeatedly pass in review, and who may select you as the object of their especial scrutiny. Dress at home, if possible; if not, go to the school early, and array yourself rapidly, but carefully, for there may be fifty riders present during the evening, and there will be little room to spare on the mounting-stand, and no minutes to waste on buttoning gloves, shortening skirt straps or tightening boot lacings. Remember all that you have been taught about mounting and about taking your reins, and think assiduously of it, with a determination to pay no attention to the gallery. There will be no spectators on the mounting-stand, and Theodore, who will take charge of you in the ring, will mount before you do, and when you have been put in your saddle by one of the masters, and start, he will take his place on your right, nearer the centre of the ring. While you are walking your horses slowly about, turning corners carefully and never ceasing to control your reins, warn him that when you say, "Centre," he must turn out to the right instantly, that you also may do so. If possible, you will not pronounce the word, but will ride as long as the horses canter or trot in time to the music.

"Do you understand," Theodore asks, "that these horses adjust their gait to the music?"

"So Nell's friend says."

"Well, I don't believe it. They are good horses, but I don't believe that they practice circus tricks. Why must I go to the centre the minute that you bid me? Why couldn't you pull up and pass out behind me?"

"Because if I did, somebody might ride over me. It is not proper to stop while on the track."

"Oh-h! How long do they trot or canter at a time? Half an hour?"

"Only a few minutes," you answer, wondering whether Theodore really supposes that you could canter, much less trot half an hour, even if stimulated by the music of the spheres.

"That's a pretty rider," he says, as a girl circles lightly past, sitting fairly well, and rising straight, but with her arms so much extended that her elbow is the apex of a very obtuse angle, though her forearms are horizontal. You explain this point to Theodore, who replies that she looks pretty, and seems to be able to trot for some time, whereupon your heart sinks within you. What will he say when he sees the necessary brevity of your performance?

Other riders enter: two or three men mounted on their own horses, beautiful creatures concerning whose value fabulous tales are told in the stable; the best rider of the school, very quietly and correctly dressed, and managing her horse so easily that the women in the gallery do not perceive that she is guiding him at all, although the real judges, old soldiers, a stray racing man or two, the other school pupils and the master—regard her admiringly, and the grooms, as they bring in new horses, keep an eye on her and her movements, as they linger on their way back to the stable.

"Her horse is very good," Theodore admits, "but I don't think much of her. Well, yes, she is pretty," he admits, as she executes the Spanish trot for a few steps and then pats her horse's shoulder; "it's pretty, but anybody could do it on a trained horse, couldn't they, sir?" he asks your master, who rides up, mounted on his own pet horse.

"Anybody who knew how. The horse has been trained to answer certain orders, but the orders must be given. An untrained horse would not understand the orders, no matter how good an animal he might be. Antinous might not have been able to ride Bucephalus, and I don't believe that Alexander could have coaxed Rosinante into a Spanish trot. It isn't enough to have a Corliss engine, or enough to have a good engineer: you must have them both, and they must be acquainted with one another. I don't believe that horse would do that for you."

"No, I don't think he would," Theodore says dryly, for he has been watching, and has reluctantly owned to himself that he does not see how the movement is effected. Meantime, you, Esmeralda, have been arduously devoting yourself to maintaining a correct attitude, and are rewarded by hearing somebody in the gallery wonder whether you represent the kitchen poker or Bunker Hill Monument.

"Don't mind," your master says, encouragingly. "It is better to be stiffly erect than to be crooked, and as for the person who spoke, she could not ride a Newfoundland dog," and with that he touches his hat, and rides lightly across the ring to speak to a lady whose horse has, in the opinion of the gallery, been showing a very bad temper, although in reality every plunge and curvet has been made in answer to her wrist and to the tiny spur which his rider wears and uses when needed. The lady nods in answer to something which the master says, the two draw near to the wall, side by side, the others fall in behind them, and the band begins a waltz, playing rather deliberately at first, but soon slightly accelerating the time.

There is very little actual need of guiding your horse, Esmeralda, because long habit has taught him what to do at a music-ride, but you do right to continue to endeavor to make him obey you. Should he stumble; should that man riding before you and struggling to make his horse change his leading foot fail in the attempt, and cause the poor creature to fall; should the rider behind you lose control of her horse, your firm hold of the reins would be of priceless value to you, but now the waltz rhythm suddenly changes to that of a march, and your horse begins to trot, slowly and with little action at first, and then with a freer, longer stride which really lifts you out of the saddle, sending you rather too high for grace, indeed, but making the effort very slight for you, and enabling you to think about your elbows, and sitting to the right and keeping your right shoulder back and your right foot close to the saddle and pointing downward, and your left knee also close, and "about seventy-five other things," as you sum up the case to yourself. Thanks to this, you are enabled to continue until the music stops, and Theodore says, approvingly, "Well, you can ride a little."

"A very little," your master says. She has learned something, of course, but it would be the unkindest of flattery for me to fell her that she does well."

# In the Riding-School: Chats With Esmeralda

"One must begin to ride in early childhood," Theodore says.

"One should begin to be taught in childhood," the master amends, "but it is not absolutely necessary. Some of the best riders in the French Army never mounted until they went to the military school, and some of the best riders at West Point only know a horse by sight until they fall into the clutches of the masters there, and then!" His countenance expresses deep commiseration.

"Now," he adds, "if you take my advice, you two, you will take places in the centre of the ring; you will sit as well as you know how, Miss Esmeralda, and you will watch the others through the next music. It is perfectly allowable," he adds, drawing rein a moment as he passes, "to sit a little carelessly when your horse is at rest, always keeping firm hold of the reins, but I would rather that you did not do it until you had ridden a little more and are firmer in your seat. Hollow your waist the least in the world, for the sake of our poker-critic in the gallery, and watch for bad riding as well as for good," and away he goes, and again the double circle of riders sweeps around the ring, and you have time to see that the horses seem to enjoy the motion, and that their action is more easy and graceful than it is when they are obeying the commands of poor riders.

Theodore indulges in a little sarcasm at the expense of a man whose elbows are on a level with his shoulders, while his two hands are within about three inches of one another on the reins, and his horse has as full possession of his head as of his body and legs, which is saying much, for his riders toes are pointing earthward and his heels apparently trying to find a way to one another through the body of his steed. Another man, riding at an amble into which he has forced his fat horse by using a Mexican bit, and keeping his wrists in constant motion; and another, who leans backward until his nose is on a level with the visor of his cap, also attract his attention, but he persists in his opinion that the best riders among the ladies are those who can trot and canter the longest, until your master, coming up, says in answer to your protest against such heresy, "No. Ease and a good seat are indeed essential, but they are not everything. They insure comfort and confidence, but not always safety. It is well to be able to leap a fence without being thrown. It is better to know how to stop and open a gate and shut it after you, lest some day you should have a horse which cannot leap, or a sprained wrist which may make the leap imprudent for yourself. You can acquire the seat almost insensibly while learning the management, but you must study in order to learn the management. However, you came mainly for enjoyment to-night, I think. Go and ride some more."

And you obey, and you have the enjoyment. And when you go to the dressing-room, it is with a feeling of perfect indifference to the gallery critics, and when you come down, ready for the street, you have a little gossip with the master.

This is the only kind of music ride, he tells you, practicable for riders of widely varying ability, but the ordinary circus is but a poor display of horsemanship compared to what may be seen in some private evening classes in this country, or in military schools. There are groups of riders in Boston and in New York, friends who have long practiced together, who can dancer the lancers and Virginia reels as easily on horseback as on foot, and who can ride at the ring as well as Lord Lindesay himself, or as well as the pretty English girls who amuse themselves with the sport in India.

"Just think," you sigh, "to be able to make your horse go forward and back, and to move in a circle, a little bit of a circle, and to do all of it exactly in time! Oh!"

And then, seeing Theodore perfectly unmoved, your master tells of the military music rides when, rank after rank, the soldiers dash across the wide spaces of the school and stop at a word, or by a preconcerted, silent signal, every horse's head in line, every left hand down, saber or lance exactly poised, every foot motionless, horse and rider still as if wrought from bronze. And then he tells of the labyrinthine evolutions when the long line moving over the school floor coils and uncoils itself more swiftly than any serpent, each horse moving at speed, each one obeying as implicitly as any creature of brass and iron moved by steam. And then he talks of broadsword fights, in which the left hand, managing the horse, outdoes the cunning of the right, and of the great reviews, when, if ever, a monarch must feel his power as he sees his squadrons dash past him, saluting as one man, and reflects on the expenditure of mental and physical power represented in that one moment's display.

"You can't learn to do such things as these," he says, "by mere rough riding. Why, only the other day, when Queen Victoria went to Sandringham, the gentlemen of the Norfolk County hunt turned out to escort her carriage, all in pink, all wearing the green velvet caps of the hunt, all splendidly mounted and perfectly appointed. They were a magnificent sight, and it was no wonder that Her Majesty looked at them with approval.

"In a dash across country they would probably have surpassed any other riders in the world, unless, perhaps, those of some other English country, but when Her Majesty and the Prince of Wales appeared at a front window, and the gentlemen rode past to salute them, what happened? The first three or four ranks went on well enough, although Frenchmen, or Spaniards, or Germans would have done better, because they, had they chosen, would have saluted and then reined backward, but the Englishmen made a gallant show, and Her Majesty smiled. Somebody raised a cheer, and the horses began to rear and perform movements not named in the school manuals. The Queen laughed outright, and the gentlemen finished their pretty parade in some confusion. Now a very little school training would have prevented that accident, and the huntsmen would have been as undisturbed as Queen Christina was that day when her horse began to plunge while in a procession, and she quickly brought him to his senses, and won the heart of every Spaniard who saw her by showing that 'the Austrian' could ride. An English hunting-man's seat is so good that he is often careless about fine details, but a trained horseman is careless about nothing, and a trained horsewoman is like unto him."

And now the lights are out, and you and Theodore go away, and, walking home, lay plans for further work in the saddle, for he, too, has caught the riding-fever, and now you begin to think about class lessons.

VIII.

All in a wow.
*Sothern.*

And you really fancy, Esmeralda, that you are ready for class lessons? You have been in the saddle only six times, remember. But you have been assured, on the highest authority, that fifty lessons in class are worth a hundred private lessons? And the same authority says that the class lessons should be preceded by at least twice as much private instruction as you have enjoyed; but, naturally, you suppress this unfavorable context. You think that you cannot begin to subject yourself to military discipline so soon?

After that highly edifying statement of your feelings, Esmeralda, hasten away to school before the dew evaporates from your dawning humility, and make arrangements for entering a class of beginners. You are fortunate in arriving half way between two "hours," and find to your delight that you may begin to ride with five or six other pupils on the next stroke of the clock, and you hasten to array yourself, and come forth just in time to see another class, a long line of pretty girls, making its closing rounds, the leader sitting with exquisitely balanced poise, which seems perfectly careless, but is the result of years of training and practice; others following her with somewhat less grace, but still accomplishing what even your slightly taught vision perceives to be feats of management far beyond you; still others, one blushing little girl with her hat slung on her arm, the heavy coils of her hair falling below her waist; and an assistant master riding with the last pupil, who is less skillful than the others, while another master rides up and down the line or stands still in the centre of the ring, criticising, exhorting, praising, using sarcasm, entreaty and sharp command, until the zeal and energy of all Gaul seem centered in his speech.

The clock strikes, and in a trice the whole class is dismounted, and its members have scampered away to make themselves presentable for the journey home, and to you, awaiting your destiny in the reception room, enter Versatilia, the beauty, and the society young lady, and Nell, and you stare at them in wrathful astonishment fully equalled by theirs, and then, in the following grand outburst of confession, you are informed that, each one having planned to outgeneral the others and to become a wondrous equestrian, the Fates and the wise fairy who, sitting in a little room overlooking the ring, presides over the destinies of classes, have willed that you should be taught together.

"And there are three other young ladies who have never ridden at all," the wise fairy says, "and they are to ride behind  you, and you must do very well in order to encourage them," she adds with a kind smile; and then there is a general muster of grooms and horses, and in a moment you are all in your saddles and walking about the ring, into which, an instant after, another lady rides easily and gracefully, to be saluted by both masters with a sigh of relief, and requested to take the lead, which she does, trotting lightly across the ring, wheeling into line and falling into a walk with trained precision, and now the lesson really begins.

"You must understand, ladies," says the teacher, that you must always, in riding in class, keep a distance of about three feet between your horse and the one before you, and that you must preserve this equally in the corners, on the short sides of the school, and on the long sides."

"That's easy enough, I'm sure," says the society young lady, taking it upon herself to answer, and eliciting an expression of astonishment from the teacher, not because he is surprised, habit already rendering him sadly familiar with young women of her type, but because he wishes to relegate her to her proper position of submissive silence as soon as may be.

"You think so?" he asks. "Then we shall depend on you to regard the distance with great accuracy. At present you are two feet too far in the rear. Forward! Now, ladies, when I say 'forward,' it is not alone for one; it is for all of you; each one must look and see whether or not her horse is in the right place. And she must not bend sideways to do it, Miss Versatilia. She must look over her horse's head between his ears. Now, forward! Now, look straight between your horse's ears, each one of you, and see something on the horse before you that is just on a line with the top of his head, and use that as a guide to tell you whether or not you are in place! Now, forward, Miss—Miss Lady! Not so fast! Keep walking! Do not let him trot! Keep up in the corners! Do not let your horse go there to think! Use your whip lightly! Not so, not so!" as the society young lady brings down her whip, half on the shoulder of gentle Toto, half on his saddle, and sets him dancing lightly out of line, to the discomfiture of Versatilia's horse, who follows him from a sense of duty.

"Take your places again," cries your teacher, "and keep to the wall! If you had had proper control of your horse, that would not have happened, Miss Versatilia! Now, Miss Lady, hold your whip in the hollow of your hand, and use it by a slight movement, not by raising your arm and lashing, lashing, lashing as if you were on the race course. A lady is not a jockey, and she should employ her whip almost as quietly as she moves her left foot. Forward, forward! And keep on the track, ladies! Keep your horses' heads straight by holding your reins perfectly even, then their bodies will be straight, and you will make one line instead of being on six lines as you are now. And, Miss Esmeralda, forward! Use your whip! Not so gently! It is not always enough to give your horse one little tap. Give him many, one after the other with quickened movement, so that he will understand that you are in a hurry. It is like the reveille which sounds ever louder until everybody is awake!

"Now, you must not make circles! Make squares! Go into the corners! Don't pull on your horse's head, Miss Nell! He thinks that you mean him to stop, and then you whip him and he tries to go on, and you pull again, and he knows not what to think. Always carry out whatever purpose you begin with your horse if you can. If sometimes you make a mistake, and cannot absolutely correct it because of those behind you, guide your horse to his proper place, and the next time that you come to that part of the ring, make him go right! Forward, forward! Ladies, not one of you is in the right place! Keep up! Keep up! Miss Lady, you must go forward regularly! Now prepare to trot! No, no! Walk! When I say, 'Prepare to trot,' it is not for you to begin, but to think of what you must do to begin, and you must not let your horses go until I give the second order, and then not too fast at first. Now, prepare to trot! Trot! Not quite so fast, Miss Lady; gently! Keep up, keep up, Miss Beauty! Miss Esmeralda, you are sitting too far to the left, your left shoulder is too far back! on't hold your hands so high, Miss Versatilia! Rise straight, Miss Esmeralda! Now, remember, ladies, what I say is for all. Prepare to whoa! Whoa!"

The leader, by an almost imperceptible series of movements, first sitting down in her saddle, then slightly relaxing her hold of the reins, and turning both hands very slightly inward, brings her horse to a walk and continues on her way. The others, with more or less awkwardness, come to a full stop, and your teacher laughs.

"When I say that," he explains, "I mean to cease trotting, not to stop. Go forward, and remember how you have been taught to go forward, Miss Esmeralda. It is not enough to frown at your horse. Now, prepare to trot! Trot!" And then he repeats again and again that series of injunctions which already seems so threadbare to you, Esmeralda, but which you do not follow, not because you do not try, but because you have not full control of your muscles, and then comes once more the order, "Prepare to whoa. Whoa!" and a volley of sharp reminders about the solemn duty of keeping a horse moving while turning corners, and once more the column proceeds as regularly as possible.

"I observe," says your teacher, riding close to you, "that you seem timid, Miss Esmeralda. Do you feel frightened."

"No," you assure him.

"Then it is because you are nervous that you are so rigid. Try not to be stiff. Give yourself a little more flexibility in the fingers, the wrists, the elbows, everywhere! You are not tired? No? Be easy then, be easy!" And you remember that you have been likened unto a poker, and sadly think that, perhaps the comparison was just.

"The other master shall ride with you for a few rounds," he continues; "that will give you confidence, and you will not be nervous." You indignantly disclaim the possession of nerves, he smiles indulgently, and the other teacher rides up beside you, and advises you steadily and quietly during the next succession of trotting and walking, and, conscious of not exerting yourself quite so much and of being easier, you begin to think that perhaps you have a nerve or two somewhere, and you determine to conquer them.

"You are sitting too far to the right now," says your new guide, the most quiet of North Britons. "There should be about half an inch of the saddle visible to you beyond the edge of your habit, if it fit quite smooth, but you would better not look down to se it. It would do no harm for once, perhaps, but it would look queer, and might come to be a habit. Try to judge of your position by the feeling of your shoulders and by thinking whether you are observing every rule; but, once in a great while, when you are walking, take your reins in your left hand, pass your right hand lightly along the edge of your saddle, ad satisfy yourself that you are quite correct in position. If you be quite sure that you can take a downward glance, without moving your head, try it occasionally, but very rarely. Use this, in fact, as you would use a measure to verify a drawing after employing every other test, and if any teacher notice you and reprove you for doing it, do not allow yourself to use it again for two or three lessons, for, unless you can be quiet about it, it is better not to use it at all."

"Ladies, ladies," cries a new voice, at the sound of which the leader is seen to sit even better than before, "this is not a church, that you should go to sleep while you are taught truth! Attend to your instructor! Keep up when he tells you. Make your movements with energy. You tire him; you tire me; you tire the good horses! how then, rouse yourselves! Prepare to trot! Trot!" And away go the horses, for it is not every hour that they hear the strong voice which means that instant obedience must be rendered. "Keep up! keep up!" cries your teacher. "Come in!" says your own guide, and then pauses himself, to urge one of the beginners behind you, and for a minute or two the orders follow one another thick and fast, the three men working together, each seeming to have eyes for each pupil, and to divine the intentions of his coadjutors, and then comes the order, "Prepare to whoa! Whoa! and the master sits down on the mounting-stand, and frees his mind on the subject of corners, a topic which you begin to think is inexhaustible.

"Please show these ladies how to go into a corner," he concludes, and your teacher does so, executing the movement so marvelously that it seems as if he would have no difficulty in performing it in any passageway through which his horse could walk in a straight line. The whole class gazes enviously, to be brought to the proper frame of mind by a sharp expostulatory fire of: "Keep your distance! Forward!" with about four times as many warnings addressed to the society young lady as to all the others; and then suddenly, unexpectedly, the clock strikes and the lesson is over.

The society young lady dresses herself with much precision and deliberation, and announces that she will never, no, never! never so long as she lives, come again; and in spite of Nell's attempts to quiet her, she repeats the statement in the reception room, in the master's hearing, aiming it straight at his quiet countenance.

"No?" he says, not so much disturbed as she could desire. "You should not despair, you will learn in time."

"I don't despair," she answers; "but I know something, and I will not be treated as if I knew nothing."

"An, you know something," he repeats, in an interested way. "But what you do not know, my young lady, is how little that something is! This is a school; you came here to be taught. I will not cheat you by not teaching you."

"And it is no way to teach! Three men ordering a class at once!"

"Ah, it is 'no way to teach'! Now, it is I who am taking a lesson from you. I am greatly obliged, but I must keep to my own old way. It may be wrong —for you, my young lady—but it has made soldiers to ride, and little girls, and other young ladies, and I am content. And these others? Are they not coming any more?"

And every one of those cowardly girls huddles away behind you, Esmeralda, and leaves you to stammer, "Y-yes, sir, but you do s-scold a little hard."

"That," says the master, "is my bog voice to make the horses mind, and to make sure that you hear it. And I told you the other day that I spoke for your good, not for my own. If I should say every time I want trotting, 'My dear and much respected beautiful young ladies, please to trot,' how much would you learn in a morning?"

"We are ladies," says the society young lady, "and we should be treated as ladies."

"And you—or these others, since you retire—are my pupils, and shall be treated as my pupils," he says with a courtly bow and a "Good morning," and you go away trying to persuade the society young lady to reconsider.

"Not that I care much whether she does or not," Nell says confidentially to you. "She's too overbearing for me," and just at that minute the voice of the society young lady is heard to call the master "overbearing," and you and Nell exchange delighted, mischievous smiles.

Now for that stiffness of yours, Esmeralda, there is a remedy, as there is for everything but death, and you should use it immediately, before the rigidity becomes habitual. Continue your other exercises, but devote only about a third as much time to them, and use the other two thirds for Delsarte movements.

First: Let your hands swing loosely from the wrist, and swing them lifelessly to and fro. Execute the movement first with the right hand then with the left, then with both.

Second: Let the fingers hang from the knuckles, and shake them in the same way and in the same order.

Third: Let the forearm hang from the elbow, and proceed in like manner.

Fourth: Let the whole arm hang from the shoulder, and swing the arms by twisting the torso.

Execute the finger and hand movements with the arms hanging at the side, extended sidewise, stretched above the head, thrust straight forward, with the arms bent at right angles to them and with the arms flung backward as far as possible. Execute the forearm movements with the arms falling at the side, and also with the elbow as high as the shoulder.

After you have performed these exercises for a few days, you will begin to find it possible to make yourself limp and lifeless when necessary, and the knowledge will be almost as valuable as the ability to hold yourself firm and steady. You will find the exercises in Mrs. Thompson's "Society Gymnastics," but these are all that you will need for at least one week, especially if you have to devote many hours to the task of persuading the society young lady not to leave your class unto you desolate.

IX.

"Left wheel into line!" and they
wheel and obey.
    *Tennyson.*

When you arrive at the school for your second class lesson, Esmeralda, you find the dressing-room pervaded by a silence as clearly indicative of a recent tempest as the path cloven through a forest by a tornado. From the shelter of screens and from retired nooks, come sounds indicative of garments doffed and donned with abnormal celerity and severity, but never a word of joking, and never a cry for deft-fingered Kitty's assistance, and then, little by little, even these noises die away, and the palace of the Sleeping Beauty could not be more quiet. No girl stirs from her lurking-place, until our yourself issue from your pet corner, and then Nell, a warning finger on her lip, noiselessly emerges from hers, and you go into the reception room together, and she explains to you that, despite her announcement that she would never come again, the society young lady has appeared, and has announced her intention to defend what she grandly terms her position as a lady.

"And the master will think us, her associates, as unruly as she is!" Nell almost sobs. "If I were he, I would send the whole class home, there!" But the other girls now enter, each magnificently polite to the others, and the file of nine begins its journey along the wall, attended as before, the society young lady taking great pains about distance, and really doing very well, but the beauty sitting with calm negligence which soon brings a volley of remonstrance from both teachers, who address her much after the fashion of Sydney Smith's saying, "You are on the high road to ruin the moment you think yourself rich enough to be careless."

"You must not keep your whip in contact with your horse's shoulder all the time," lectured one of the teachers, "if you do, you have no means of urging him to go forward a little faster. Keep it pressed against the saddle, not slanting outward or backward. When you use it, do it without relaxing your hold upon the reins, for if, by any mischance, your horse should start quickly, you will need it. Forward, ladies, forward! don't stop in the corners! Use your whips a very little, just as you begin to turn! Miss Esmeralda, keep to the wall! No, no! Don't keep to the wall by having your left rein shorter than your right! They should be precisely even."

"As you approach the corner," says the other teacher quietly, speaking to you alone, "carry your right hand a little nearer to your left without bending your wrist, so that your rein will just touch your horse's neck on the right side. That will keep his head straight."

"But he seems determined to go to the right," you object.

"That is because your right rein is too short now. While we are going down the long side of the school, make the reins precisely even. Now, lay the right rein on his neck, use your whip, and touch him with your heel to make him go on; bend your right wrist to turn him, use your whip once more, and go on again!"

"Forward, Miss Esmeralda, forward!" cries the other teacher.

"That is because Miss Lady did not go into the corner, and so is too far in advance," your teacher explains. "You must, in class, keep your distance as carefully when the rifer immediately before you is wrong as when she is right. It is the necessity of doing that, of having to be ready for emergencies, to think of others as much as of your horse and of yourself, that give class teaching much of its value."

"Forward, ladies, forward," cries the other teacher. "Remember that you are not to go to sleep! Now prepare to trot, and don't go too fast at first. Remember always to change from one gait to another gently, for your own sake, that you may not be thrown out of position; for your horse's, that he may not be startled, and made unruly and ungraceful. He has nerves as well as you. Now, prepare to trot! Trot! Shorten your reins, Miss Beauty! Shorten them!" and during the next minute or two, while the class trots about a third of a mile, the poor beauty hears every command in the manual addressed to her, and smilingly tries, but tries in vain to obey them; but in an unhappy moment the teacher's glance falls on the society young lady and he bids her keep her right shoulder back. "You told me that before," she says, rather more crisply than is prescribed by any of he manuals of etiquette which constitute her sole library.

"Then why don't you do it?" is his answer. "Keep your left shoulder forward," he says a moment later, whereupon the society young lady turns to the right, and plants herself in the centre of the ring with as much dignity as is possible, considering that her horse, not having been properly stopped, and feeling the nervous movements of her hands, moves now one leg and now another, now draws his head down pulling her forward on the pommel, and generally disturbs the beautiful repose of manner upon which she prides herself.

"You are tired? No? Frightened? Your stirrup is too short? You are not comfortable?" demands the teacher, riding up beside her. "Is there anything which you would like to have me do?"

"I don't like to be told to do two things at once," she responds in a tone which should be felt by the thermometer at the other end of the ring.

"But you must do two things at once, and many more than two, on horseback," he says; "when you are rested, take your place in the line."

"I think I will dismount," she says.

"Very well," and before she has time to change her mind, a bell is rung, a groom guides her horse to the mounting-stand, the master himself takes her out of the saddle, courteously bids her be seated in the reception room and watch the others, and she finds her little demonstration completely and effectually crushed, and, what is worse, apparently without intention. Nobody appears to be aware that she has intended a rebellion, although "whole Fourth of Julys seem to bile in her veins."

"Now," the teacher goes on, "we will turn to the right, singly. Turn! Keep up, ladies! Keep up! Ride straight! To the right again! Turn!" and back on the track, on the other side of the school, the leader in the rear, the beginners in advance, you continue until two more turns to the right replace you.

"That was all wrong," the teacher says, cheerfully. "You did not ride straight, and you did not ride together. Your horses' heads should be in line with one another, and then when you arrive at the track and turn to the right again, your distance will be correct. Now we will have a little trot, and while you are resting afterward, you shall try the turn again."

The society young lady, watching the scene in sulkiness, notes various faults in each rider and feels that the truly promising pupil of the class is sitting in her chair at that moment; but she says nothing of the kind, contenting herself by asking the master, with well-adjusted carelessness, if it would not be better for the teacher to speak softly.

"It gives a positive shock to the nerves to be so vehemently addressed," she says, with the air of a Hammond advising an ignorant nurse.

"That is what he has the intention to do," replies the other. "It is necessary to arouse the rider's will and not let her sleep, but if it were not, the teacher of riding, or anybody who has to give orders, orders, orders all day long, must speak from an expanded chest, with his lungs full of air, or at night he will be dumb. The young man behind the counter who has to entreat, persuade, to beg, to be gentle, he may make his voice soft, but to speak with energy in a low tone is to strain the vocal cords and to injure the lungs permanently. The opera singer finds to sing piano, pianissimo more wearisome than to make herself heard above a Wagner orchestra. The orator, with everybody still and listening with countenance intent, dares not speak softly, except now and then for contrast. In the army we have three months' rest, and then we go to the surgeon, and he examines our throats and lungs, and sees whether or not they need any treatment. If you go to the camp of the military this summer, you will find the young officers whom you know in the ball-room so soft and so gentle, not whispering to their men, but shouting, and the best officer will have the loudest shout."

The society young lady remembers the stories which she has heard her father and uncles tell of that "officer's sore throat," which in 1861 and 1862, caused so many ludicrous incidents among the volunteer soldiery, the energetic rill master of one day being transformed into a voiceless pantomimist by the next, but, like Juliet when she spoke, she says nothing, and now the teacher once more cries, "Turn!" and then, suddenly, "Prepare to stop! Stop! Now look at your line! Now two of you have your horses' heads even! And how many of you were riding straight?"

A dead silence gives a precisely correct answer, and again he cries, "Forward!" A repetition of the movement is demanded, and is received with cries of "This is not good, ladies! This is not good! We will try again by and by. Now, prepare to change hands in file."

The leader, turning at one corner of the school, makes a line almost like a reversed "s" to the corner diagonally opposite, and comes back to the track on the left hand, the others straggling after with about as much precision and grace as Jill followed Jack down the hill; but, before they are fairly aware how very ill they have performed the manoeuvre, they perceive that their teacher not only aimed at having them learn how to turn to the left at each corner, but also at giving himself an opportunity to make remarks about their feet and the position thereof, and at the end of five minutes each girl feels as if she were a centipede, and you, Esmeralda, secretly wonder whether something in the way of mucilage of thumb-tacks might not be used to keep your own riding boots close to the saddle. "And don't let your left foot swing," says the teacher in closing his exhortations; "hold it perfectly steady! Now change hands in file, and come back to the track on the right again, and we will have a little trot."

"And before you begin," lectures the master, "I will tell you something. The faster you go, after once you know how to stay in the saddle, the better for you, the better for your horse. You see the great steamer crossing the ocean when under full headway, and she can turn how this way and now that, with the least little touch of the rudder, but when she is creeping, creeping through the narrow channel, she must have a strong, sure hand at the helm, and when she is coming up to her wharf, easy, easy, she must swing in a wide circle. That is why my word to you is always 'Forward! Forward!' and again, 'Forward!' There is a scientific reason underlying this, if you care to know it. When you go fast, neither you nor the horse has time to feel the pressure of the atmosphere from above, and that is why it seems as if you were flying, and he is happy and exhilarated as well as you. You will see the tame horse in the paddock gallop about for his pleasure, and the wild horse on the prairie will start and run for miles in mere sportiveness. So, if you want to have pleasure on horseback, 'Forward!'"

While the little trot is going on, the society young lady improves the shining hour by asking the master "if he does not think it cruel to make a poor horse go just as fast as it can," to which he replies that the horse will desire to go quite as long as she can or will, whereupon she withdraws into the cave of sulkiness again, but brightens perceptibly as you dismount and join her.

"You do look so funny, Esmeralda," she begins. "Your feet do seem positively immense, as the teacher said."

"Pardon me; I said not that," gently interposes the teacher; "only that they looked too big, bigger than they are, when she turns them outward."

"And you do sit very much on one side," she continues to Versatilia: "and your crimps are quite flat, my dear," to the beauty.

"Never mind; they aren't fastened on with a safety pin," retorts the beauty, plucking up spirit, unexpectedly.

"O, no! of course not," the wise fairy interposes, with a little laugh. "You young ladies do not do such things, of course. But, do you know, I heard of a lady who wore a switch into a riding-school ring one day, and it came off, and the riding master had to keep it in his pocket until the end of the session."

Little does the wise fairy know of the society young lady's ways! What she has determined to say, she declines to retain unsaid, and so she cries: "And you do thrust your head forward so awkwardly, Nell!"

"'We are ladies,'" quotes Nell, "and we can't answer you," and the society young lady finds herself alone with the wise fairy, who is suddenly very busy with her books, and after a moment, she renews her announcement that she is not coming any more. "Well, I wouldn't," the wise fairy says, looking thoughtfully at her. "You make the others unhappy, and that is not desirable, and you will not be taught. I gave you fair warning that the master would be severe, but those who come here to learn enjoy their lessons. Once in a great while there are ladies who do not wish to be taught, but they find it out very soon, as you have."

"There is always a good reason for everything," the master says gravely. "Now, I have seen many great men who could not learn to ride. There was Gambetta. Nothing would make a fine rider out of that man! Why? Because for one moment that his mind was on his horse, a hundred it was on something else. And Jules Verne! He could not learn! And Emile Giardin! They had so many things to think about! Now, perhaps it is so with this young lady. Society demands so much, one must do so many things, that she cannot bend her mind to this one little art. It is unfortunate, but then she is not the first!" And with a little salute he turns away, and the society young lady, much crosser than she was before he invented this apology for her, comes into the dressing room and—bids you farewell? Not at all! Says that she is sorry, and that she knows that she can learn, and is going to try. "And I suppose now that nothing will make her go!" Nell says, lugubriously, as you saunter homeward.

You are still conscious of stiffness, Esmeralda? That is not a matter for surprise or for anxiety. All your life you have been working for strength, for even your dancing-school teacher was not one of those scientific ballet-masters who, like Carlo Blasis, would have taught you that the strength of a muscle often deprives it of flexibility and softness. You desire that your muscles should be rigid or relaxed at will. Go and stand in front of your mirror, and let your head drop forward toward either shoulder, causing your whole torso to become limp. Now hold the head erect, and try to reproduce the feeling. The effect is awkward, and not to be practised in public, but the exercise enables you to perceive for yourself when you are stiff about the shoulders and waist. Now drop your head backward, and swing the body, not trying to control the head, and persist until you can thoroughly relax the muscles of the neck, a work which you need not expect to accomplish until after you have made many efforts. Now execute all your movements for strengthening the muscles, very slowly and lightly, using as little force as possible. After you can do this fairly well, begin by executing them quickly and forcibly, then gradually retard them, and make them more gently, until you glide at last into perfect repose. This will take time, but the good results will appear not only in your riding, but also in your walking and in your dancing. You and Nell might practise these Delsarte exercises together, for no especial dress is needed for them, and companionship will remove the danger of the dulness which, it must be admitted, sometimes besets the amateur, unsustained by the artist's patient energy. Before you take another class lesson, you may have an exercise ride, in which to practise what you have learned. "Tried to learn!" do you say? Well, really, Esmeralda, one begins to have hopes of you!

## X.

—Ye couldn't have made him a rider,
And then ye know, boys will be boys, and hosses,
— well, hosses is hosses!
*Harte.*

When you and Nell go to take your exercise ride, Esmeralda, you must assume the air of having ridden before you were able to walk, and of being so replete with equestrian knowledge that the "acquisition of another detail would cause immediate dissolution," as the Normal college girl said when asked if she knew how to teach. You must insist on having a certain horse, no matter ho much inconvenience it may create, and, if possible, you should order him twenty-four hours in advance, stipulating that nobody shall mount him in the interval, and, while waiting for him to be brought from the stable, you should proclaim that he is a wonderfully spirited, not to say vicious, creature, but that you are not in the smallest degree afraid of him. You should pick up your reins with easy grace, and having twisted them into a hopeless snarl, should explain to any spectator who may presume to smile that one "very soon forgets the little things, you know, but they will come back in a little while."

Having started, you must choose between steadily trotting or rapidly cantering, absolutely regardless of the rights or wishes of any one else, or else you must hold your horse to a spiritless crawl, carefully keeping him in such a position as to prevent anybody else from outspeeding you. If you were a man, you would feel it incumbent on you to entreat your master to permit you to change horses with him, and would give him certain valuable information, derived from quarters vaguely specified as "a person who knows," or "a man who rides a great deal." meaning somebody who is in the saddle twenty times a year, and duly pays his livery stable bill for the privilege, and you would confide in some other exercise rider, if possible, in the hearing of seven or eight pupils, that your master was not much of a rider after all, that the "natural rider is best," and you would insinuate that to observe perfection it was only necessary to look at you. If, in addition to this, you could intimate to any worried or impatient pupils that they had not been properly taught, you would make yourself generally beloved, and these are the ways of the casual exercise rider, male and female. But you, Esmeralda, are slightly unfitted for the perfect assumption of this part by knowing how certain things ought to be done, although you cannot do them, and alas! you are not yet adapted to the humbler but prettier character of the real exercise rider, who is thoroughly taught, and whose every movement is a pleasure to behold.

There are many such women and a few men who prefer the ring to the road for various reasons, and from them you may learn much, both by observation and from the hints which many of them will give you if they find that you are anxious to learn, and that you are really nothing more pretentious than a solitary student. So into the saddle you go, and you and Nell begin to walk about in company. "In company," indeed, for about half a round, and then you begin to fall behind. Touching your Abdallah lightly with whip and heel starts him into a trot and coming up beside Nell you start off her Arab, and both horses are rather astonished to be checked. What do these girls want, they think, and when you fall behind again, it takes too strokes of the whip to urge Abdallah forward, Arab is unmoved by your passing him, and you find the breadth of the ring dividing you and Nell. You pause, she turns to the right, crosses the space between you, turns again and is by your side, and now both of you begin to see what you must do. Nell, who is riding on the inside, that is to say on the included square, must check her horse very slightly after turning each corner, and you must hasten yours a little before turning, and a little after, so as to give her sufficient space to turn, and, at the same time, to keep up with her. You, being on her left, must be very careful every moment to have a firm hold of your left rein, so as to keep away from her feet, and she must keep especial watch of her right rein in order to guard herself.

After each of you has learned her part pretty well, you should exchange places and try again, and then have a round or two of trotting, keeping your horses' heads in line. You will find both of them very tractable to this discipline, because accustomed to having your master's horse keep pace with them, and because they often go in pairs at the music rides, and you must not expect that an ordinary livery stable horse would be as easily managed. It is rather fashionable to sneer at the riding-school horse as too mild for the use of a good rider, and very likely, while you and Nell are patiently trying your little experiment, you will hear a youth with very evident straps on his trousers, superciliously requesting to have "something spirited" brought in from the stable for him.

"Not one of your school horses, taught to tramp a treadmill round, but a regular flyer," he explains.

"Is he a very good rider?" you ask your master. "Last time he was hear I had to take him off Abdallah," he says sadly, and then he goes to the mounting-stand to deny "the regular flyer," and to tender instead, "an animal that we don't give to everybody, William." Enter "William," otherwise Billy Buttons, whom the gentleman covetous of a flyer soon finds to be enough for him to manage, because William, although accustomed to riders awkward through weakness, is not used to the manners of what is called the "three-legged trotter"; that is to say, the man whose unbent arms and tightened reins make a straight line from his shoulders to his horse's mouth, while his whole weight is thrown upon the reins by a backward inclination of his body.

If you would like to know how Billy feels about it, Esmeralda, bend your chin toward your throat, and imagine a bar of iron placed across your tongue and pulling your head upward. It would hurt you, but you could raise your head and still go forward, making wild gestures with your hands, kicking, perhaps, in a ladylike manner, as Gail Hamilton kicked Halicarnassus, but by no means stopping. Now suppose that bar of iron drawn backward by reins passing one on each side of your shoulders and held firmly between your scapulae; you could not go forward without almost breaking your neck, could you? No more could Billy, if his rider would let out his reins, bend his elbows, and hold his hands low, almost touching his saddle, but, as it is, he goes on, and if he should rear by and by, and if his rider should slide off, be not alarmed. The three-legged trotter is not the kind of horseman to cling to his reins, and he will not be dragged, and Billy is too good-tempered not to stop the moment he has rid himself of his tormentor. But while he is still on Billy's back, and flattering himself that he is doing wonders in subjugating the "horse that we don't give to everybody," do you and Nell go to the centre of the ring and see if you can stop properly. Pretty well done, but wait a moment before trying it again, for it is not pleasant to a horse. Sit still a few minutes, and then try and see if you can back your horse a step or two.

In order to do this, it is not enough to sit up straight and to say "back," or even to say "bake," which, according to certain "natural riders," is the secret of having the movement executed properly. You must draw yourself up and lean backward, touching your horse both with your foot and with your whip, in order that he may stand squarely, and you must raise your wrists a little, and the same time turning them inward. The horse will take a step, you must instantly sit up straight, lower your hands, and then repeat the movement until he has backed far enough. Four steps will be quite as many as you should try when working thus by yourself, because you do not wish to form any bad habits, and your master will probably find much to criticise in your way of executing the movement. The most that you can do for yourself is to be sure that Abdallah makes but one step for each of your demands. If he make two, lower your hands, and make him go forward, for a horse that backs unbidden is always troublesome and may sometimes be dangerous.

"Just watch that man on Billy Buttons," says your master, coming up to you, "and make up your minds never to do anything that you see him do. And look at those two ladies who are mounting now, and see how well it is possible to ride without being taught in school, provided one rides enough. They cannot trot a rod, but they have often been in the saddle half a day at a time in Spanish America, whence they come, and they can 'lope,' as they call it, for hours without drawing rein. They sit almost, but not quite straight, and they have strength enough in their hands to control any of our horses, although they complain that these English bits are poor things compared to the Spanish bit. You see, they can stay on, although they cannot ride scientifically."

"And isn't that best?" asked Nell.

"It is better," corrects the master. "The very best is to stay on because one rides scientifically, and that is what I hope that you two will do by and by. There's that girl who always brings in bags of groceries for her horse! Apples this time!"

"Isn't it a good thing to give a horse a tidbit of some kind after a ride?" asked Nell.

"'Good,' if it be your own horse, but not good in a riding-school. It tends to make the horses impatient for the end of a ride, and sometimes makes them jealous of one another at the mounting-stand, and keeps them there so long as to inconvenience others who wish to dismount. Besides, careless pupils, like that girl, have a way of tossing a paper bag into the ring after the horse has emptied it, and although we always pick it up as soon as possible, it may cause another horse to shy. A dropped handkerchief is also dangerous, for a horse is a suspicious creature and fears anything novel as a woman dreads a mouse."

What is the trouble on the mounting-stand? Nothing, except that a tearful little girl wants "her dear Daisy; she never rides anything else, and she hates Clifton, and does not like Rex and Jewel canters, and she wants Da-a-isy!"

"But is it not better for you to change horses now and then, and Daisy is not fit to be in the ring to-day," says your master. "Jewel is very easy and good-tempered. Will you have him?"

"No, I'll have Abdallah."

"A lady is riding him."

"Well, I want him."

It is against the rules for your master to suggest such a thing to you, Esmeralda, but suppose you go up to the mounting-stand and offer to take Jewel yourself and let her have Abdallah. You do it; your master puts you on Jewel, and sends the wilful little girl away on Abdallah, and then comes up to you and Nell, thanks you, and says, "It was very good of you, but she must learn some day to ride everything, and I shall tell her so, and next time!"

He looks capable of giving her Hector, Irish Hector, who is wilful as the wind, but in reward for your goodness he bestows a little warning about your whips upon Nell, who has a fancy for carrying hers slantwise across her body, so that both ends show from the back, and the whole whip is quite useless as far as the horse is concerned, although picturesque enough with its loop of bright ribbon.

"It makes one think of a circus picture," he says; "and, Miss Esmeralda, don't hold your whip with the lash pointing outward, to tickle Miss Nell's horse, and to make you look like an American Mr. Briggs 'going to take a run with the Myopias, don't you know.' Isn't this a pretty horse?"

"Well, I don't know," you say frankly; "I'm no judge. I don't know anything about a horse."

For once your master loses his self-possession, and stares unreservedly. "Child," he says, "I never, never before saw anybody in this ring who didn't know all about a horse."

"Well, but I really don't, you know."

"No, but nobody ever says so. Now just hear this new pupil instruct me."

The new pupil, who thinks a riding habit should be worn over two or three skirts, and is consequently sitting with the aerial elegance of a feather bed, is riding with her snaffle rein, the curb tied on her horse's neck, and is clasping it by the centre, allowing the rest to hang loose, so that Clifton, supposing that she means to give him liberty to browse, is looking for grass among the tan. Not finding it, he snorts occasionally, whereupon she calls him "poor thing," and tells him that "it is a warm day, and that he should rest, so he should!"

"Your reins are too long," says your master.

"Do you mean that they are too long, or that I am holding them so as to make them too long," she inquires, in a precise manner.

"They are right enough. Our saddlers know their business. But you are holding them so that you might as well have none. Shorten them, and make him bring his head up in its proper place."

"But I think it's cruel to treat him so, when he's tired, poor thing! I always hold my reins in the middle when I'm driving, and my horse goes straight enough. This one seems dizzy. He goes round and round."

"He wouldn't if he were in harness with two shafts to keep his head straight" —

"But then why wouldn't it be a good thing to have some kind of a light shaft for a beginner's horse?"

"It would be a neat addition to a side saddle," says your master, "but shorten your reins. Take one in each hand. Leave about eight inches of rein between your hands. There!  See. Now Guide your horse."

He leaves her, in order that he may enjoy the idea of the side saddle with shafts, and she promptly resumes her old attitude which she feels is elegant, and when Clifton wanders up beside Abdallah, she sweetly asks Nell, "Is this your first lesson? Do you think this horse is good? The master wants me to pull on my reins, but I think it is inhuman, and I won't, and" —but Clifton strays out of hearing, and your arouse yourselves to remember that you are having more fun than work.

There is plenty of room in the ring, now, so you change hands, and circle to the left, first walking and then trotting, slowly at first, and then rapidly, finding to your pleasant surprise, that, just as you begin to think that you can go no further, you are suddenly endowed with new strength and can make two more rounds. "A good half mile," your master says, approvingly, as you fall into a walk and pass him, and then you do a volte or two, and one little round at a canter, and then walk five minutes, and dismount to find the rider of the alleged William assuring John, the head groom, that redoubtable animal needs "taking down."

"Shall ride him with spurs next time," he says. "I can manage him, but he would be too much for most men," and away he goes and a flute-voiced little boy of eight mounts William, retransformed into Billy Buttons, and guides him like a lamb, and you escape up stairs to laugh. But you have no time for this before the merciful young woman enters to say that she is going to another school, where she can do as she pleases and have better horses, too, and the more you and Nell assure her that there is no school in which she can learn without obedience, and that her horse was too good, if anything, the more determined she becomes, and soon you wisely desist.

As she departs, "Oh, dear," you say, "I thought there was nothing but fun at riding-school, and just see all these queer folks."

"My dear," says philosophic Nell, "they ar part of the fun. And we are fun to the old riders; and we are all fun to our master."

Here you find yourselves enjoying a bit of fun from which your master is shut out, for three or four girls come up from the ring together, and, not seeing you, hidden behind your screens, two, in whom you and Nell have already recognized saleswomen from whom you have more than once bought laces, begin to talk to overawe the others.

"My deah," says one, "now I think of it, I weally don't like the setting of these diamonds that you had given you last night. It's too heavy, don't you think?"

The other replies in a tone which would cheat a man, but in which you instantly detect an accent of surprise and a determination to play up to her partner as well as possible, that she "liked it very well."

"I should have them reset," says the former speaker. "Like mine, you know; light and airy. Deah me, I usedn't to care for diamonds, and now I'm puffectly infatooated with them, don't you know! My!" she screams, catching sight of a church clock, and, relapsing into her everyday speech: "Half-past four! And I am due at" —[An awkward pause.] "I promised to return at four!"

There is no more talk about diamonds, but a hurried scramble to dress, an a precipitate departure, after which one of the other ladies is heard to say very distinctly: "I remember that girl as a pupil when I was teaching in a public school, and I know all about her. Salary, four dollars a week. Diamonds!"

"She registered at the desk as Mrs. Something," rejoins the other. "She only came in for one ride, and so they gave her a horse without looking up her reference, but one of the masters knew her real name. Poor little goosey! She has simply spoiled her chance of ever becoming a regular pupil, no matter how much she may desire it. No riding master will give lessons to a person who behaves so. He would lose more than he gained by it, no matter how long she took lessons. And they know everybody in a riding-school, although they won't gossip. I'd as soon try to cheat a Pinkerton agency."

"I know one thing," Nell says, as you walk homeward: "I'm going to take an exercise ride between every two lessons, and I'm going to ride a new horse every time, if I can get him, and I'm going to do what I'm told, and I shall not stop trotting at the next lesson, even if I feel as if I should drop out of the saddle. I've learned so much from an exercise ride."

XI.

Ride as though you were flying.
*Mrs. Norton.*

"Cross," Esmeralda? Why? Because having had seven lessons of various sorts, and two rides, you do not feel yourself to be a brilliant horsewoman? Because you cannot trot more than half a mile, and because you cannot flatter yourself that it would be prudent for you to imitate your favorite English heroines, and to order your horse brought around to the hall door for a solitary morning canter? And you really think that you do well to be angry, and that, had your teacher been as discreet and as entirely admirable as you feel yourself to be, you would be more skilful and better informed?

Very well, continue to think so, but pray do not flatter yourself that your mental attitude has the very smallest fragment of an original line, curve or angle. Thus, and not otherwise, do all youthful equestrians feel, excepting those doubly-dyed in conceit, who fancy that they have mastered a whole art in less than twelve hours. You certainly are not a good rider, and yet you have received instruction on almost every point in regard to which you would need to know anything in an ordinary ride on a good road. You have not yet been taught every one of these things, certainly, for she who has been really taught a physical or mental feat, can execute it at will, but you have been partly instructed, and it is yours to see that the instruction is not wasted, by not being either repeated, or faithfully reduced to practice. Remember clever Mrs. Wesley's answer to the unwise person who said in reproof, "You have told that thing to that child thirty times." "Had I told it but twenty-nine," replied the indomitable Susanna, "they had been wasted." What you need now is practice, preferably in the ring with a teacher, but if you cannot afford that, without a teacher, and road rides whenever you can have them on a safe horse, taken from a school stable, if possible, with companions like yourself, intent upon study and enjoyment, not upon displaying their habits, or, if they be men, the airs of their horses, and the correctness of their equipment, or upon racing.

As for the solitary canter, when the kindly Fates shall endow that respectable American sovereign, your father, with a park somewhat bigger than the seventy-five square feet of ground inclosed by an iron railing before his present palace, it will be time enough to think about that; but you can no more venture upon a public road alone than an English lady could, and indeed, your risk in doing so would be even greater than hers. Why? Because in rural England all men and boys, even the poorest and the humblest, seem to know instinctively how a horse should be equipped. True, a Wordsworth or a Coleridge did hesitate for hours over the problem of adjusting a horse collar, but Johnny Ragamuffin, from the slums, or Jerry Hickathrift, of some shire with the most uncouth of dialects, can adjust a slipping saddle, or, in a hand's turn, can remove a stone which is torturing a hoof.

Not so your American wayfarer, city bred or country grown; it will be wonderful if he can lengthen a stirrup leather, ad, before allowing such an one to tighten a girth for you, you would better alight and take shelter behind a tree, and a good large tree, because he may drive your horse half frantic by his well-meant unskilfulness. Besides, Mrs. Grundy very severely frowns on the woman who rides alone, and there is no appeal from Mrs. Grundy's wisdom. Sneer at her, deride her, try, if you will, to undermine her authority, but obey her commands and yield to her judgment if you would have the respect of men, and, what is of more consequence, the fair speech of women. And so, Esmeralda, as you really have no cause for repining, go away to your class lesson, which has a double interest for you and Nell, because of the wicked pleasure which you derive from hearing the master quietly crush the society young lady with unanswerable logic.

You have seen him with a class of disobedient, well-bred little girls, and know how persuasive he can be to a child who is really frightened. You have seen him surrounded by a class of eager small goys, and beset with a clamorous shout of, "Plea-ease let us mount from the ground." You have heard his peremptory "No," and then, as they turned away discomfited, have noted how kindly was his "I will tell you why, my dear boys. It is because your legs are too short.

Wait until you are tall, then you shall mount." You know that when Versatilia, having attended a party the previous evening and arisen at five o'clock to practise Chopin, and then worked an hour at gymnastics, could not, from pure weariness, manage her horse, how swift was his bound across the ring, and how carefully he lifted her from the saddle, and gave her over to the ministrations of the wise fairy. You know that any teacher must extract respect from his scholars, and you detect method in all the little sallies which almost drive the society young lady to madness, but this morning it is your turn.

You do, one after the other, all the things against which you have been warned, and, when corrected, you look so very dismal and discouraged that the Scotch teacher comes quietly to your side and rides with you, and, feeling that he will prevent your horse from doing anything dangerous, you begin to mend your ways, when suddenly you hear the master proclaim in a voice which, to your horrified ears, seems audible to the whole universe: "Ah, Miss Esmeralda! she cannot ride, she cannot do her best, unless she has a gentleman beside her." In fancy's eye you seem to see yourself blushing for that criticism during the remainder of your allotted days, and you almost hope that they will be few. You know that every other girl in the class will repeat it to other girls, and even to men, and possibly even to Theodore, and that you will never be allowed to forget it. Cannot ride or do your best without a gentleman, indeed! You could do very well without one gentleman whom you know, you think vengefully, and then you turn to the kindly Scotch teacher, and, with true feminine justice, endeavor to punish him for another's misdeeds by telling him that, if he please, you would prefer to ride alone. As he reins back, you feel a decided sinking of the heart and again become conscious that you are oddly incapable of doing anything properly, and then, suddenly, it flashes upon you that the master was right in his judgment, and you fly into a small fury of determination to show him that you can exist "without a gentleman." Down go your hands, you straighten your shoulders, adjust yourself to a nicety, think of yourself and of your horse with all the intensity of which you are capable, and make two or three rounds without reproof.

"Now," says the teacher, "we will try a rather longer trot than usual, and when any lady is tired she may go to the centre of the ring. Prepare to trot! Trot!"

The leader's eyes sparkle with delight as she allows her good horse, after a round or two, to take his own speed, the teacher continues his usual fire of truthful comments as to shoulders, hands and reins, and one after another, the girls leave the track, and only the leader and you remain, she, calm and cool as an iceberg, you, flushed, and compelled to correct your position at almost every stride of your horse, sometimes obliged to sit close for half a round, but with your whole Yankee soul set upon trotting until your master bids you cease. Can you believe your ears?

"Brava, Miss Esmeralda!" shouts the master. "Go in again. That is the way. Ah, go in again! That is the way the rider is made! Again! Ah, brava!"

"Prepare to whoa! Whoa!" says the teacher, and both he and your banished cavalier congratulate you, and it dawns upon you that the society young lady is not the only person whom the master understands, and is able to manage. However, you are grateful, and even pluck up courage to salute him when next you pass him; but alas! that does not soften his heart so thoroughly that he does not warningly ejaculate, "Right foot," and then comes poor Nell's turn. She, reared in a select private school for young ladies, and having no idea of proper discipline, ventures to explain the cause of some one of her misdeeds, instead of correcting it in silence. She does it courteously, but is met with, "Ah-h-h! Miss Esmeralda, you know Miss Nell. Is it not with her on foot as it is on horseback? Does she not argue?"

You shake your head severely and loyally, but brave Nell speaks out frankly, "Yes, sir; I do. But I won't again."

"I would have liked to ride straight at him," she confides to you afterwards, "but he was right. Still, it is rather astounding to hear the truth sometimes."

And now, for the first time around, you are allowed to ride in pairs, and the word "interval," meaning the space between two horses moving in parallel lines, is introduced, and you and Nell, who are together, congratulate yourselves on having in your exercise ride learned something of the manner in which the interval may be preserved exactly, for it is a greater trouble to the others than that "distance" which you have been told a thousand times to "keep." You have but very little of this practice, however, before you are again formed in file, and directed to "Prepare to volte singly!"

When this is done perfectly, it is a very pretty manoeuvre, and, the pupils returning to their places at the same movement, the column continues on its way with its distances perfectly preserved, but as no two of your class make circles of the same size, or move at similar rates of speed, your small procession finds itself in hopeless disorder, and in trying to rearrange yourselves, each one of you discovers that she has yet something to learn about turning. However, after a little trot and the usual closing walk, the lesson ends, and you retire from the ring, with the exception of Nell, who, having been taught by an amateur to leap in a more or less unscientific manner, has begged the master to give her "one little lesson," a proposition to which he has consented.

The hurdle is brought out, placed half-way down one of the long sides of the school, and Nell walks her horse quietly down the other, turns him again as she comes on the second long side, shakes her reins lightly, putting him to a canter, and is over—"beautifully," as you say to yourself, as you watch her enviously.

"You did not fall off," the master comments, coiling the lash of the long whip with which he has stood beside the hurdle during Miss Nell's performance, "but you did not guard yourself against falling when you went up, and had you had some horses, you might have come down before he did, although that is not so easy for a lady as it is for a man. When you start for a leap, you must draw your right foot well back, so as to clasp the pommel with your knee, and just as the horse stops to spring upward, you must lean back and lift both hands a little, and then, when he springs, straighten yourself, feel proud and haughty, if you can, and, as he comes down, lean back once more and raise your hands again, because your horse will drop on his fore legs, and you desire him to lift them, that he may go forward before you do. You should practise this, counting one, as you lean backward, drawing but not turning the hands backward and upward; two, as you straighten yourself wit the hands down, and three, as you repeat the first movement; and, except in making a water jump, or some other very long leap, the 'two' will be the shortest beat, as it is in the waltz. And, although you must use some strength in raising your hands, you must not raise them too high, and you must not lean your head forward or draw your elbows back. A jockey may, when riding in a steeplechase for money, but he will be angry with himself for having to do it, and a lady must not. I would rather that you did not leap again to-day, because what I told you will only confuse you until you have time to think it over and to practise it by yourself in a chair. And I would rather that you did not leap again in your own way, until you have let me see you do it once or twice more, at least."

"You did not have to whip my horse to make him leap," Nell says,

"The whip was not to strike him, but to show him what was ready for him if he refused," says the master. "One must never permit a horse to refuse without punishing bum, for otherwise he may repeat the fault when mounted by a poor rider, and a dangerous accident may follow. One must never brutalize a horse—indeed, no one but a brute does—but one must rule him."

By this time he has taken Nell from her saddle and is in the reception room where he finds you grouped and gazing at him in a manner rather trying even to his soldierly gravity, and decidedly amusing to the wise fairy, who glances at him with a laugh and betakes herself to her own little nest.

"My young ladies," he says. "I will show you one little leap, not high, you know, but a little leap sitting on a side saddle," and, going out, he takes Nell's horse, and in a minute you see him sailing through the air, light as a bird, and without any of the encouraging shouts used by some horsemen. It is only a little leap, but it impresses your illogical minds as no skilfulness in the voltes and no *haute ecole* airs could do, for leaping is the crowning accomplishment of riding in the eyes of all your male friends except the cavalryman, and when he returns to the reception room, you linger in the hope of a little lecture, and you are not disappointed.

"My young ladies," he says, "at the point at which you are in the equestrian art, what you should do is to keep doing what you know, over and over again, no matter if you do it wrong. Keep doing and doing, and by and by you will do it right. I have tried that plan of perfecting each step before undertaking another, but it is of no use with American ladies. You will not do things at all, unless you can do them well, you say. That is to say if you were to go to a ball, and were to say, 'No, I have taken lessons, I have danced in school, but I am afraid I cannot do so well as some others. I will not dance here.' That would not be the way to do. Dance, and again dance, and if you make a little mistake, dance again! The mistake is of the past; it is not matter for troubling; dance again, and do not make it again. And so of riding, ride, and again ride! Try all ways. Take your foot out of the stirrup sometimes, and slip it back again without stopping your horse, and when you can do it at the walk, do it at the trot, and keep rising! And learn not to be afraid to keep trotting after you are a little tired. Keep trotting! Keep trotting! Then you will know real pleasure, and you will not hurt your horses, as you will if you pull them up just as they begin to enjoy the pace. And then"—looking very hard at nothing at all, and not at you, Esmeralda, as your guilty soul fancies—"and then, gentlemen will not be afraid to ride with you for fear of spoiling their horses by checking them too often."

And with this he goes away, and on! Esmeralda, does not the society young lady make life pleasant for you and Nell in the dressing-room, until the beauty attracts general attention by stating that she has had an hour of torment!

"Perhaps you have not noticed that most of these saddles are buckskin," she continues; "I did not, until I found myself slipping about on mine to day as if it were glazed, and lo! It was pigskin, and that made the difference. I would not have it changed, because the Texan is always sneering at English pigskin, and I wanted to learn to ride on it; but, until the last quarter of the hour, I expected to slip off. I rather think I should have," she adds, "only just as I was ready to slip off on one side, something would occur to make me slip to the other. I shall not be afraid of pigskin again, ad you would better try it, every one of you. Suppose you should get a horse from a livery stable some day with one of those slippery saddles!"

"I am thinking of buying a horse," says the society young lad; "but the master says that I do not know enough to ride a beast that has been really trained. Fancy that!"

"And all the authorities agree with him," says Versatilia, who has accumulated a small library of books on equestrianism since she began to take lessons. "Your horse ought not to know much more than you do—for if he do, you will find him perfectly unmanageable."

Here you and Nell flee on the wings of discretion. The daring of the girl! To tell the society young lady that a horse may know more than she does!

## XII.

Costly thy habit as thy purse can buy.
*Shakespeare.*

And now, Esmeralda, having determined to put your master's advice into practice and to "keep riding," you think that you must have a habit in order to be ready to take to the road whenever you have an opportunity, and to be able to accompany Theodore, should he desire to repeat your music-ride? And you would like to know just what it will cost, and everything about it? And first, what color can you have?

You "can" have any color, Esmeralda, and you "can" have any material, for that matter. Queen Guinevere wore grass green silk, and if her skirt were as long as those worn by Matilda of Flanders, Norman William's wife, centuries after, her women must have spent several hours daily in mending it, unless she had a new habit for every ride, or unless the English forest roads were wider than they are to-day. But all the ladies of Arthur's court seem to have ridden in their ordinary dress. Enid, for instance, was arrayed in the faded silk which had been her house-dress and waking-dress in girlhood, when she performed her little feat of guiding six armor-laden horses. Queen Elizabeth and Mary Stuart seem to have liked velvet, either green or black, and to have adorned it with gold lace, and both probably took their fashions form France; the young woman in the Scotch ballad was "all in cramoisie"; Kate Peyton wore scarlet broadcloth, but secretly longed for purple, having been told by a rival, who had probably found her too pretty for scarlet, that green or purple was "her color."

There are crimson velvet and dark blue velvet and Lincoln green velvet habits without end in fiction, and in the records of English royal wardrobes, but, beautiful as velvet is, and exquisitely becoming as it would be, you would better not indulge your artistic taste by wearing it. It would cost almost three times as much as cloth; it would be nearly impossible to make a well fitting modern skirt of it, and it would be worn into ugliness by a very few hours of trotting. Be thankful, therefore, that fashion says that woollen cloth is the most costly material that may be used.

In India, during the last two or three seasons, Englishwomen have worn London-made habits of very light stuffs, mohairs and fine Bradford woollens, and there is no reason why any American woman should not do the same. In Hyde Park, for three summers, in those early morning hours when some of the best riders go, attended by a groom, to enjoy something more lively than the afternoon parade, skirts of light tweed and covert coats of the same material worn over white silk shirts, with linen collars and a man's tie, have made their wearers look cool and comfortable, and duck covert jackets, with ordinary woollen skirts have had a similar effect, but American women have rather hesitated as to adopting these fashions, lest some one, beholding, should say that they were not correct. Thus did they once think that they must wear bonnets with strings in church, no matter what remonstrance was made by the thermometer, or how surely they were deafened to psalm and sermon by longing for the cool, comfortable hats, which certain wise persons had decided were too frivolous for the sanctuary.

New York girls have worn white cloth habits at Lenox without shocking the moral sense of the inhabitants, but Lenox, during the season, probably contains a smaller percentage of simpletons than any village in the United States, and some daring Boston girls have appeared this year in cool and elegant habits of shepherd's check, and have pleased every good judge who has seen them. If quite sure that you have as much common sense and independence as these young ladies, imitate them, but if not, wear the regulation close, dark cloth habit throughout the year, be uncomfortable, and lose half the benefit of your summer rides from becoming overheated, to say nothing of being unable to "keep trotting" as long as you could if suitably clothed for exercise. But might you not, if your habit were thin, catch cold while your horse was walking? You might if you tried, but probably you would not be in a state so susceptible to that disaster as you would if heavily dressed.

There is little danger that the temperature will change so much during a three hours' ride that you cannot keep yourself sufficiently warm for comfort and for safety, and if you start for a long excursion, you must use your common sense. The best and least expensive way of solving the difficulty is to have an ordinary habit, with the waist and skirt separate, and to wear a lighter coat, with a habit shirt, or with a habit shirt and waistcoat, whenever something lighter is desirable. This plan gives three changes of dress, which should be enough for any reasonable girl.

But still, you do not know what color you can wear? Black is suitable for all hours and all places, even for an English fox hunt, although the addition of a scarlet waistcoat, just visible at the throat and below the waist, is desirable for the field. Dark blue, dark green, dark brown are suitable for most occasions, and a riding master whose experience has made him acquainted with the dress worn in the principal European capitals, declares his preference for gray with a white waistcoat.

Among the habits shown by English tailors at the French exhibition of 189, was one of blue gray, and a Paris tailor displayed a tan-colored habit made with a coat and waistcoat revealing a white shirt front. London women are now wearing white waistcoats and white ties in the Park, both tie and waistcoat as stiff and masculine as possible.

This affectation of adopting men's dress, when riding, is comparatively modern. Sir Walter gives the date in "Rob Roy," when Mr. Francis sees Diana for the first time and notices that she wears a coat, vest and hat resembling those of a man, "a mode introduced during my absence in France," he says, "and perfectly new to me." But this coat had the collar and wide sharply pointed lapels and deep cuffs now known as "directoire," and its skirts were full, and so long that they touched the right side of the saddle, and skirts, lapels, collar and cuffs were trimmed with gold braid almost an inch wide. The waistcoat, the vest, as Sir Walter calls it, not knowing the risk that he ran in this half century of being considered as speaking American, had a smaller, but similar, collar and lapels, work outside those of the coat, and the "man's tie" was of soft white muslin, and a muslin sleeve and ruffles were visible at the wrists. The hat was very broad brimmed, and was worn set back from the forehead, and bent into coquettish curves, and altogether the fair Diana might depend upon having a very long following of astonished gazers if she should ride down Beacon Street or appear in Central Park to-day.

Your habit shall not be like hers, Esmeralda, but shall have a plain waist, made as long as you can possibly wear it while sitting, slightly pointed in front and curving upward at the side to a point about half an inch below that where the belt of your skirt fastens, and having a very small and perfectly flat postilion, or the new English round back. Elizabeth of Austria may wear a princess habit, if it please her, but would you, Esmeralda, be prepared, in order to have your habit fit properly, to postpone buttoning it until after you were placed in the saddle, as she was accustomed to do in the happy days when she could forget her imperial state in her long wild gallops across the beautiful Irish hunting counties? The sleeves shall not be so tight that you can feel them, nor shall the armholes be so close as to prevent you from clasping your hands above your head with your arms extended at full length, and the waist shall be loose. If you go to a tailor, Esmeralda, prepare yourself to make a firm stand on this point. Warn him, in as few words as possible, that you will not take the habit out of his shop unless it suits you, and do not allow yourself to be overawed by the list of his patrons, all of whom "wear their habits far tighter, ma'am." Unless you can draw a full, deep breath with your habit buttoned, you cannot do yourself or your teacher any credit in trotting, and you will sometimes find yourself compelled to give your escort the appearance of being discourteous by drawing rein suddenly, leaving him, unwarned, to trot on, apparently disregarding your plight. Both your horse and his will resent your action, and unless he resemble both Moses and Job more strongly than most Americans, he will have a few words to say in regard to it, after you have repeated it once or twice. And, lastly, Esmeralda, no riding master with any sense of duty will allow you to wear such a habit in his presence without telling you his opinion of it, and stating his reasons for objecting to it, and you best know whether or not a little lecture of that sort will be agreeable, especially if delivered in the presence of other women. Warn your tailor of your determination, then, and if his devotion to his ideal should compel him to decline your patronage, go to another, until you find one who will be content not to transform you into the likeness of a wooden doll. Women are not made to advertise tailors, whatever the tailors may think.

What must you pay for your habit? You may pay three hundred dollars, if you like, although that price is seldom charged, unless to customers who seem desirous of paying if, but the usual scale runs downward from one hundred and fifty dollars. This includes cloth and all other materials, and finish as perfect within as without, and is not dear, considering the retail price of cloth, the careful making, and the touch of style which only practised hands can give. The heavy meltons worn for hunting habits in England cost seven dollars a yard; English tweeds which have come into vogue during the last few years in London, cost six dollars, broadcloth five dollars; rough, uncut cheviots, about six dollars; and shepherds' checks, single width, about two dollars and a half. For waistcoats, duck costs two dollars and a quarter a yard, and fancy flannels and Tattersall checks anywhere from one dollar and a half to two dollars. The heavy cloths are the most economical in the end, because they do not wear out where the skirt is stretched over the pommel, the point at which a light material is very soon in tatters.

The small, flat buttons cost twenty-five cents a dozen; the fine black sateen used for linings may be bought for thirty-five cents a yard, and canvas for interlinings for twenty-five cents. With these figures you may easily make your own computations as to the cost of material, for unless a woman is "more than common tall," two yards and a half will be more than enough for her habit skirt, which should not rest an inch on the ground on the left side when she stands, and should not be more than a quarter of a yard longer in its longest part. Two lengths, with allowance for the hem two inches deep are needed for the skirt, and when very heavy melton is used, the edges are left raw, the perfect riding skirt in modern eyes being that which shows no trace of the needle, an end secured with lighter cloths by pressing all the seams before hemming, and then very lightly blind-stitching the pointed edges in their proper place.

Strength is not desirable in the sewing of a habit skirt. It is always possible that one may be thrown, and the substantial stitching which will hold one to pommel and stirrup may be fatal to life. So hems are constructed to tear away easily, and seams are run rather than stitched, or stitched with fine silk, and the cloth is not too firmly secured to the wide sateen belt. The English safety skirts, invented three or four years ago, have the seam on the knee-gore open from the knee down to the edge, and the two breadths are caught together with buttons and elastic loops, all sewed on very lightly so as to give way easily. The effect of this style of cutting is, if one be thrown, to transform one into a flattered or libelous likeness of Lilian Russell in her naval uniform, prepared to scamper away from one's horse, and from any other creatures with eyes, but with one's bones unbroken and one's face unscathed by being dragged and pounded over the road, or by being kicked.

For the waist and sleeves, Esmeralda, you will allow as much as for those of your ordinary frocks, and if you cannot find a fashionable tailor who will consent to adapt himself to your tastes and to your purse, you may be fortunate enough to find men who have worked in shops, but who now make habits at home, charging twenty-five dollars for the work, and doing it well and faithfully, although, of course, not being able to keep themselves informed as to the latest freaks of English fashion by foreign travellers and correspondents, as their late employers do. There are two or three dressmakers in Boston and five or six in New York whose habits fit well, and are elegant in every particular, and, if you can find an old-fashioned tailoress who really knows her business, and can prepare yourself to tell her about a few special details, you may obtain a well-fitting waist and skirt at a very reasonable price.

Of these details the first is that the sateen lining should be black. Gay colors are very pretty, but soon spoiled by perspiration, and white, the most fitting lining for a lady's ordinary frock, is unsuitable for a habit, since one long, warm ride may convert it into something very untidy of aspect. This lining, of which all the seams should be turned toward the outside, should end at the belt line, and between it and the cloth outside should be a layer of canvas, cut and shaped as carefully as possible, and the whalebones, each in its covering, should be sewed between the canvas and the sateen. If a waistcoat be worn, it should have a double sateen back with canvas interlining, and may be high in the throat or made with a step collar like that of the waist. The cuffs are simply indicated by stitching and are buttoned on the outside of the sleeve with two or three buttons. Simulated waistcoats, basted firmly to the shoulder seams and under-arm seams of the waist, and cut high to the throat with an officer collar, are liked by ladies with a taste for variety, and are not expensive, as but for a small quantity of material is required for each one. They are fastened by small hooks except in those parts shown by the openings, and on these flat or globular pearl buttons are used.

When a step collar and a man's tie are worn, the ordinary high collar and chemisette, sold for thirty-eight cents, takes the place of the straight linen band worn with the habit high in the throat, and the proper tie is the white silk scarf fastened in a four-in-hand knot, and, if you be wise, Esmeralda you will buy this at a good shop, and pay two dollars and a quarter for it, rather than to pay less and repent ever after. Some girls wear white lawn evening ties, but they are really out of place in the saddle, in which one is supposed to be in morning dress. Wear the loosest of collars and cuffs, and fasten the latter to your habit sleeves with safety pins. The belts of your habit skirt and waist should also be pinned together at the back, at the sides, and the front, unless your tailor has fitted them with hooks and eyes, and if you be a provident young person, you will tuck away a few more safety pins, a hairpin or two, half a row of "the most common pin of North America," and a quarter-ounce flash of cologne, in one of the little leather change pouches, and put it either in your habit pocket or your saddle pocket. Sometimes, after a dusty ride of an hour or two, a five-minute halt under the trees by the roadside, gives opportunity to remove the dust from the face and to cool the hands, and the cologne is much better than the handkerchief "dipped in the pellucid waters of a rippling brook," *a la* novelist, for the pellucid brook of Massachusetts is very likely to run past a leather factory, in which case its waters are anything but agreeable. Whether or not your habit shall have a pocket is a matter of choice. If it have one, it should be small and should be on the left side, just beyond the three flat buttons which fasten the front breadth and side breadth of your habit at the waist. When thus placed, you can easily reach it with either hand.

Fitting the habit over the knee is a feat not to be effected by an amateur without a pattern, and the proper slope and adjustment of the breadths come by art, not chance; but Harper's Bazaar patterns are easily obtained by mail. The best tailors adjust the skirt while the wearer sits on a side saddle, and there is no really good substitute for this, for, although one my guess fairly well at the fir of the knee, nothing but actual trial will show whether or not, when in the saddle, the left side of the skirt hangs perfectly straight, concealing the right side, and leaving the horse's body visible below it. When your skirt is finished, no matter if it be made by the very best of tailors, wear it once in the school before you appear on the road with it, and, looking in the mirror, view it "with a crocket's eye," as the little boy said when he appeared on the school platform as an example of the advantages of the wonderful merits of oral instruction.

An elastic strap about a quarter of a yard long should be sewed half way between the curved knee seam and the hem, and should be slipped over the right toe before mounting, and a second strap, for the left heel, should be sewed on the last seam on the under side of the habit, to be adjusted after the foot is placed in the stirrup. The result of this cutting and arrangement is the straight, simple, modern habit which is so great a change from the riding dress of half a century ago, with its full skirt which nearly swept the ground. The short skirt first appears in the English novel in "Guy Livingstone," and is worn by the severe and upright Lady Alice, the dame who hesitated not to snub Florence Bellasis, when snubbing was needful, and who was a mighty huntress. Now everybody wears it, and the full skirts are seen nowhere except in the riding-school dressing-rooms, where they yet linger because they may be worn by anybody, whereas the plain skirts fits but one person. It seems odd that so many years were required to discover that a short skirt, held in place by a strap placed over the right toe and another slipped over the left heel, really protected the feet more than yards of loosely floating cloth, but did not steam and electricity wait for centuries? Since the new style was generally adopted, Englishwomen allow themselves the luxury of five or six habits, instead of the one or two formerly considered sufficient, but each one is worn for several years. When the extravagant wife, in Mrs. Alexander's "A Crooked Path," suggests that she may soon want a new habit, her husband asks indignantly, "Did I not give you one two years ago?"

The trousers may mach the habit or may be of stockinet, or the imported cashmere tights may be worn. Women who are not fat and whose muscles are hard, may choose whichsoever one of these pleases them, but fat women, and women whose flesh is not too solid, must wear thick trousers, and would better have them lined with buckskin, unless they would be transformed into what Sairey would call "a mask of bruiges," and would frequent remark to Mrs. Harris that such was what she expected. Trousers with gaiter fastenings below the knee are preferred by some women who put not their faith in straps alone, and knee-breeches are liked by some, but to wear knee breeches means to pay fifteen dollars for long riding-boots, instead of the modest seven or eight dollars which suffice to buy ordinary Balmoral boots. Gaiters must button on the left side of each leg, and trouser straps may be sewed on one side and buttoned on the other, instead of being buttoned on both sides as men's are. Tailors sometimes insist on two buttons, but as a woman does not wear her trousers except with the strap, it is not difficult to see why she needs to be able to remove it. The best material for the strap is thick soft kid, or thin leather lined with cloth. The thick, rubber strap used by some tailors is dangerous, sometimes preventing the rider from placing her foot in the stirrup, sometimes making her lose it at a critical moment. Whether breeches, tights, or trousers are worn, they must be loose at the knee, or trotting will be impossible, and the rider will feel as if bound to the second pommel, and will sometimes be unable to rise at all.

As to gloves, the choice lies between the warm antelope skin mousquetaires at two dollars a pair, and the tan-colored kid gauntlets at the same price. The former are most comfortable for winter, the latter for summer, and neither can be too large. Nobody was ever ordered out for execution for wearing black gloves, although they are unusual, and now and then one sees a woman, whose soul is set on novelty, gorgeous in yellow cavalry gauntlets, or even with white dragoon gauntlets, making her look like a badly focused photograph.

Lastly, as to the hat. What shall it be, Esmeralda?

No tuft of grass-green plumes for you, like Queen Guinevere's, nor yet the free flowing feather to be seen in so many beautiful old French pictures, nor the plumed hat which "my sweet Mistress Ann Dacre" wore when Constance Sherwood's loving eyes first fell upon her, but the simple jockey cap, exactly matching your habit, and costing two dollars and a half or three dollars; the Derby cap for the same price or a little more; or, best of all, the English or the American silk hat, as universally suitable as a black silk frock was in the good old times when Mrs. Rutherford Birchard Hayes was in the White House. The English Henry Heath hat at seven or eight dollars, with its velvet forehead piece and its band of soft, rough silk, stays in place better than any other, but it is too heavy for comfort. If you can have an American hatter remodel it, making it weigh half a pound less, it will be perfection, always provided that he does not, as he assuredly will unless you forbid it, throw away the soft, rough band, which keeps the hat in place, and substitute one of the American smooth bands, designed to slip off without ruffling the hair, and doing it instantly, the moment that a breeze touches the brim of the hat. A hunting guard, fastened at the back of the hat brim and between two habit buttons is better than an elastic caught under the braids of your hair, for when an elastic does not snap outright, it is always trying to do so, and in the effort holds the hat so tightly on the head so as sometimes to give actual pain. The hunting guard is no restraint at all unless the hat flies off, in which case it keeps it from following the example of John Gilpin's, but with the Henry Heath lining, your hat is perfectly secure in anything from a Texas

Norther to a New England east wind. If you follow London example, and wear a straw hat for morning rides, sew a piece of white velvet on the inner side of the band, and your forehead will not be marked.

Arrayed after these suggestions, Esmeralda, you will be inconspicuous, and that is the general aim of the true lady's riding dress, with the exception of those worn by German princesses, when, at a review, they lead the regiments which they command. Then, their habits may be frogged and braided with gold, or they may fire the air in habit and hat of white and scarlet, the regimental colors, as the Empress of Germany did the other day. If you were sure of riding as these royal ladies do, perhaps even white and scarlet might be permitted to you, but can you fancy yourself, Esmeralda, sweeping across a parade ground with a thousand horsemen behind you, and ready to salute your sovereign and commander-in-chief at the right moment, and to go forward with as much precision as if you, too, were one of those magnificently drilled machines brought into being by the man of blood and iron?

## XIII.

'Tis an old maxim in the schools,
That flattery's the food of fools.
    *Swift.*

If American children and American girls were the angels which their mothers and their lovers tell them that they are, the best possible riding master for them would be an American soldier who had learned and taught riding at West Point. Being of the same race, pupil and teacher would have that vast fund of common memories, hopes and feelings; that common knowledge of character, of good qualities and of defects, and that ability to divine motives and to predict action which constitute perfect sympathy, and their relations to one another would be mutually agreeable and profitable. Unfortunately, Esmeralda, you, like possibly some other American girls, are not an angel, and if you were, you could not have such a riding master, because the very few men who have the specified qualifications are too well acquainted with the characteristics of their countrywomen to instruct them in the equestrian art. Who, then, shall be his substitute? Clearly, either a person sufficiently patient and clever to neutralize the faults of American women, or one capable of adapting himself to them, of eluding them, and of forcing a certain quantity of knowledge upon his pupils, almost in spite of themselves. The former is hardly to be found among natives of the United States; the latter can be found nowhere else, except, possibly, in certain English shires in which the inhabitants so closely resemble the average American that when they immigrate hither they are scarcely distinguishable from men whose ancestors came two or three centuries ago.

A foreign teacher, whether French, German, or Hungarian, always regards himself in the just and proper European manner as the superior of his pupil. The traditions in which he has been reared, in which he has been instructed, not only in riding, but in all other matters, survive from the time when all learning was received from men whose title to respect rested not only on their wisdom but on their ecclesiastical office, and who expected and received as much deference from their pupils as from their congregations. Undeniably, there are unruly children in European schools, but their rebelliousness is never encouraged, and their teachers are expected to quell it, not to submit to it, much less to endeavour to avoid it by giving no commands which are distasteful. Even in the worst conducted private schools on the continent, there is always at least one master who must be obeyed, whose authority is held as beyond appeal, and in the school conducted either by the church or by civil authority, the duty of enforcing perfect discipline is regarded as quite as imperative as that of demanding well-learned lessons.

Passing through these institutions, the young European enters the military school with as little thought of disputing any order which may be given him as of arguing with the priest who states a theological truth from the pulpit. And, indeed, had he been reared under the tutelage of one of those modern silver-tongued American pedagogues, who make gentle requests lest they should elicit antagonism by commands, the military school should soon completely alter the complexion of his ideas, for he would find his failures in the execution of orders treated as disobedience. He would not be punished at first, it is true, but pretty theories that he was nervous, or ill, or the victim of hereditary disability, or of fibre too delicately attenuated to perform any required act, would not be admitted except, indeed, as a reason for expulsion. Moreover, the tests to which he would be compelled to submit before this escape from discipline lay open to him, would be neither slight nor easily borne, for the European military teacher has yet to learn the existence of that exquisite personal dignity which is hopelessly blighted by corporal punishment or infractions of discipline.

"Will you teach me how to ride, sir?" asked a Boston man of a Hungarian soldier, one of the pioneers among Boston instructors.

"Will I teach you! Eh! I don't know," said the exile dolefully, for during his few weeks in the city, he had seen something of the ways of the American who fancies himself desirous of being taught. "Perhaps you will learn, but will—I—teach—you? You can ride?"

"A little."

"Very well! Mount that horse, and ride around the ring."

Away went the pupil, doing his best, but before he had traversed two sides of the school, the master shouted to the horse, and the pupil was sitting in the tan. He picked himself up, and returned to the mounting-stand, saying: "Will you tell me how to stay on next time?"

"I will," cried the Hungarian in a small ecstasy; "and I will make a rider of you!" And he did, too, and certainly took as much pleasure in his pupil in the long course of instruction which followed, and in the resultant proficiency.

In European riding-schools for ladies, there is, of course, no resort to corporal punishment, but there is none of that careful abstention from telling disagreeable truths which popular ignorance extracts from American teachers in all schools, except in the military and naval academies. Indeed, the need of it is hardly felt, for that peculiar self-consciousness which makes an American awkward under observation and restive under reproof is scarcely found in countries not democratic, and the "I'm ez good ez you be" feeling that is at the bottom of American intractability, has no chance to flourish in lands where position is a matter of birth and not of self-assertion.

A French woman, compelled to make part of her toilet in a railway waiting-room under the eyes of half a score of enemies, that is to say, of ten other women, arranges her tresses, purchased or natural, uses powder-puff and hare's foot if she choose, and turns away from the mirror armed for conquest; but an American similarly situated, forgets half her hair-pins, does not dare to wash her face carefully lest some one should sniff condemnation of her fussiness, and looks worse after her efforts at beautifying. A French girl, told that her English accent is bad, corrects it carefully; an American, gently reminded that a French "u" is not pronounced like "you," changes it to "oo," and stares defiance at Bocher and all his works. And even that commendable reserve which hinders well-bred Americans from frank self-discussion, stands in the way of perfect sympathy between him and the European master, representative of races in which everybody, from an emperor in his proclamations to the peasant chatting over his beer or *petit vin*, may discourse upon his most recondite peculiarities.

For all these reasons, the European riding master is often misunderstood, even by his older pupils, and young girls almost invariably mistake his patient reiteration and his methodical vivacity for anger, so that his classes seldom contain any pupils not really anxious to learn, or whose parents are not determined that they shall learn in his school and no other. Teaching is a matter of strict conscience with him, and even after years of experience, and in spite of more than one severe lesson as to American sensitiveness, he continues to speak the truth. Even when his pupils have become what the ordinary observer calls perfect riders, he allows no fault to go unreproved, although nobody can more thoroughly enjoy the evening classes, organized by fairly good riders rather for amusement than for instruction. If you think you can endure perfect discipline and incessant plain speaking go to him, Esmeralda.

If you cannot, take the other alternative, the American or the English master, but remember that it is only by absolute submission that you will obtain the best instruction which he is capable of giving. If you do not compel him to tax his mind with remembering all your foibles and weaknesses, you may, thanks to race sympathy, learn more rapidly at first from him than from a foreigner, and, unless you are rude and insubordinate to the point of insolence, you may depend upon receiving no actual harshness from him, although he will refuse to flatter you, and will repeat his warnings against faults, quite as persistently as any foreigner.

A very little observation of your fellow pupils will show you that presumption upon his good nature is wofully common, and that his American inability to forget that a woman is a woman, even when she conducts herself as if her name were Ursa or Jenny, often subjects him to stupendous impertinence, which he receives with calm and silent contempt. You will find that his instruction follows the same lines as that of all foreign masters in the United States, for there is no American system of horsemanship, the traditions of the army, and of the north, being derived from France, those of the south fro, England, and those of the southwest from Spain, by the way of Mexico and Texas. Under his instruction, you will remain longer in the debatable land between perfect ignorance of horsemanship, and being a really accomplished rider, than you would if taught by a foreigner, but, as has already been said, you will learn more rapidly at first, an the result, if you choose to work hard, will be much the same.

Should you, by way of experiment, choose to take lessons from both native and foreign masters, you will find each frankly ready to admit the merits of the other, and to acknowledge that he himself is better suited to some pupils than to others and, to come back to what was told you at the outset, you will find them unanimous in assuring you that your best teacher, the instructor without whose aid you can learn nothing, is yourself, your slightly rebellious, but withal clever, American self. You can learn, Esmeralda. There is no field of knowledge into which the American woman has attempted to enter, in which she has not demonstrated her ability to compete, when she chooses to put forth all her energy, with her sisters of other nations, but she must work, and must work steadily. There are American teachers of grammar who cannot parse; American female journalists who cannot write; American women calling themselves doctors, but unable to make a diagnosis between the cholera and the measles; and American women practising law and dependent for a living on blatant self-advertising, but with the faculties of Vassar and Wellesley in existence; with the editor of Harper's Bazar receiving the same salary as Mr. Curtis; with American women acknowledged as a credit to the medical and to the legal profession—what of it? The American woman can learn anything, can do anything. Do you learn to ride, and, having done it, "keep riding." At present you have received just sufficient instruction to qualify you to ride properly escorted, on good roads, but —

"KEEP RIDING!"

Lightning Source UK Ltd.
Milton Keynes UK
UKHW010638310521
384676UK00001B/93